365

AMAZING
QUESTIONS
& ANSWERS

Curious and quirky questions
answered for your
reading satisfaction

9 Why is Stalin known as a mysterious person ?

To begin with Stalin was not his real name. It was Josef Vissarionovich Djugashvili. He picked Stalin as a name because the word means 'Man of Steel'. His date of birth is unknown as well. Records say 18th December, 1979, while the Russian calendar puts it at the 6th of December. Allegedly, Stalin changed it further to 21st December, 1881. Apparently, this was to avoid being tracked by the officers of the Tsars. This made him a man of mystery.

10 What are the Fabergé eggs ?

Fabergé eggs are precious, bejewelled, ornamental eggs that were made by the jeweller Fabergé on the orders of Czar Alexander III, for his wife the Czarina Marie Feodorovna. These eggs were an Easter present from the Czar to his wife. The first egg that Fabergé made was very simple and looked like a real egg but on opening it, it revealed a golden yolk which also opened to show a golden hen. This little golden hen also split open to display the imperial crown from which hung a ruby pendant on a golden chain that the Czarina could wear around her neck.

After the first one, the Czar gave Fabergé free reign to design the Easter eggs every year as long as they were egg-shaped, had a surprise and didn't repeat a previous design.

11 Why did Hitler have such a peculiar moustache?

Hitler's moustache is famous all over the world. Few others with a similar moustache, were the comedians Charlie Chaplin and of course the ever famous Oliver Hardy. But why did Hitler have such a peculiar taste when it came to facial hair? Was it just his odd sense of fashion, or was it his way of standing out and distinguishing himself from other people? The answer is, neither. The toothbrush moustache was never Hitler's choice of facial hair style. In fact, it is said, he used to have a huge handlebar moustache. However, he had to cut and trim it in order to be able to wear a gas mask. The large handlebar moustache would stick out of the sides of the gas mask creating a gap through which any poisonous gas could easily reach the wearer's nose and respiratory system. Thus, Hitler ended up having a small rectangular patch of moustache under his nose. In 1918, he was temporarily blinded in a mustard gas attack. This makes you wonder if the trimming of his moustache really helped. One thing is certain however, the toothbrush moustache will forever be associated with Hitler!

12 Which was the longest war fought in history ?

The longest war fought in history was between the Netherlands and the Isles of Sicily. It was a war that went on for an epic 335 years!

The origins of this war can be traced to the English Civil War in 1651, between the supporters of King Charles I and those of the Parliament, led by Oliver Cromwell.
The Dutch sided with the Parliament in this conflict and had cornered the Royalist Navy at the Isles of Sicily when Dutch Admiral Maarten Tromp declared war on them. The only thing is, we don't know if he had the authority. In any case, within three months, the Royalist Navy surrendered and everyone went home, but they never signed a peace treaty, leaving us a 335-year-long war without any casualties.

13 What was the shortest war fought in history ?

9:02 WAR BEGINS
British Navy attacks

9:40 WAR ENDS

The shortest war fought in history was between the British Empire and the Sultan of Zanzibar in 1896.

Sultan Hamad of Zanzibar was loyal to the British Empire and served the Queen. However, after mere three years of his rule, he was murdered by his cousin, Khalid bin Barghash.

Khalid declared himself Sultan and unfurled his flag in Zanzibar and started preparing his own army and navy with arms and weaponry that were gifted to Zanzibar by the British over the years. The British Navy asked him to step down and after a final ultimatum, chief diplomat Basil Cave declared war on Zanzibar which lasted all of 38 minutes! About 500 people lost their lives or were injured between 9:02 and 9:40. However, British rule was re-established.

14 Did Einstein ever enter politics?

The thing about geniuses is that they are so lost in their own research, and the love for their subject that they seldom have time for anything else, let alone politics. However, Theoretical Physicist Albert Einstein came very close to becoming the second President of Israel way back in 1952.

The First President at that time was Chaiz Weizmann. Then, Chief Minister Ben Gurion, issued a letter to Einstein asking him to consider taking up the position of President. The letter asked Einstein if he was interested in the Presidency, and if he accepted, he would be expected to move to Israel and would be issued citizenship of the country. The letter further stated that he would still be allowed to pursue his passion in scientific work.

Einstein, however, declined the offer. His reply to this letter said that he was deeply ashamed that he couldn't accept the offer. He considered himself inexperienced and lacking the 'natural aptitude' required to deal with people.

One cannot help but wonder what would have happened if Einstein had accepted the offer and what impact it would have had on the history of the world.

Einstein's formula

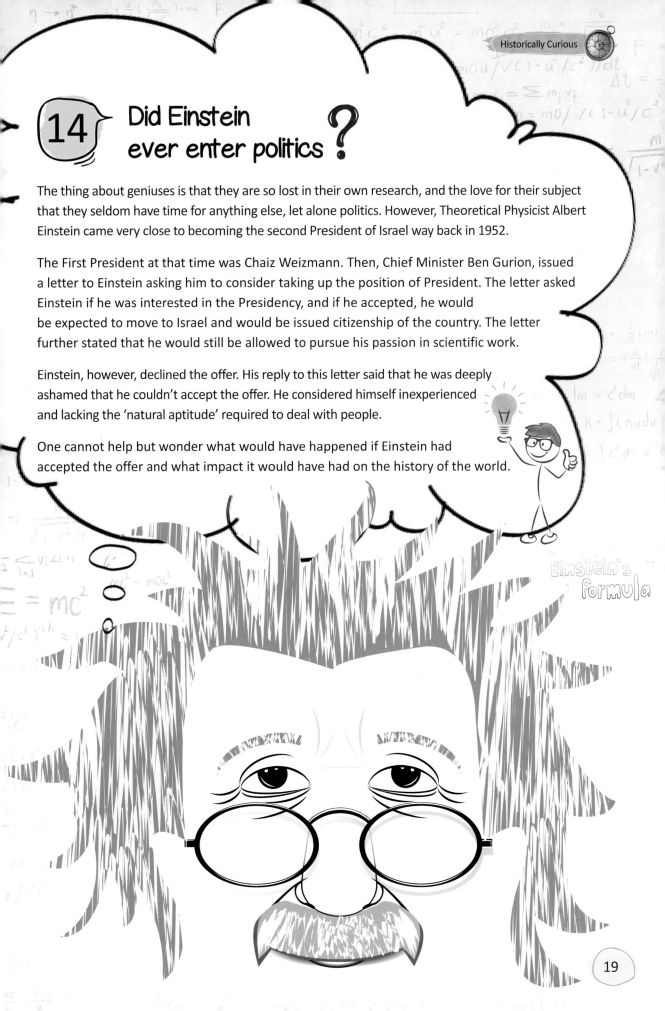

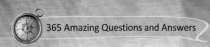

15 — Which was Napoleon's most shameful defeat ?

To celebrate the Treaty of Tilsit with the French empire, Napoleon announced a celebratory rabbit hunt. The party began prowling the grassy fields for rabbits as caged rabbits all around its periphery were let loose. Unfortunately, instead of running away, these rabbits headed straight towards the hunters, taking the party by storm! Napoleon and his guests had to retreat and were rid of the rabbits only after they got away on their carriages.

Actually, the rabbits trapped for the hunt were domestic and hence, when they saw the hunters, they thought that their food was being served, making them head straight for the hunters.

Quite shameful for Napoleon, isn't it?

16 — How did orphanages raise money back in the day ?

The usual way to raise money was and is to host a social event or plan something interactive where a majority of the people can participate. Orphanages in olden days mostly thrived on charity, either directly from the people or from the church. Many churches had their own orphanages and schools.

However, there is one fund raising event in history that will remain the weirdest way to raise money. This was an orphanage in Paris. In the year 1912, they held a lottery of live babies, where the winner received a baby from the orphanage. The Foundling Hospital made inquiries into the background of the foster parents/winners before giving away the babies for adoption.

WON A BABY!

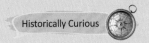

17 What does the term 'D-Day' stand for ?

'D-Day' was a term coined during World War II. However, as with all things over a certain period of time, the term has come to be used under different circumstances. Hence, there are many explanations for the expression.

The first explanation is simple. D stands for day. Just like H stands for hour, and M stands for minute. The US Army used it to denote a day of an important event, like an attack or a military move. Days before or after would then be addressed as D-1 or D+1.

The second explanation is that D in D-Day stands for 'disembarkation' or 'debarkation', specifying a pre-known date when the event of offloading cargo from a ship or airplane would be denoted. This could also be a sly way of saying 'dropping a bomb or a missile'. In such a case, the message passed from one military personnel to another would be something like, 'Troops mobilise on D-2 day.' In this way, even if it were intercepted by an enemy, they would remain clueless about its meaning.

The third explanation is that D-Day simply stands for the day of decision. This could be a day when an important decision regarding an attack, or the execution of one out of many plans is to be carried out. Usually in military strategy, many plans and back-up plans are made and the person in authority uses one of these plans at the last minute. This day would be denoted as D-Day.

18 How did Athens get its name ?

Poseidon and Athena were competing to name the city of Athens after them and be its guardian. Zeus, asked both to present a gift to the new city. The citizens would then decide whose gift was better, and that god would earn the right to name it.

Poseidon the god of water struck a rock and a spring of water emerged from it. So, his gift to the city was water and success on all sea explorations and wars.

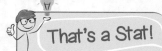

That's a Stat!

Greeks were the inventors of theatre. They loved it so much that most cities had one. Some were so big, they could hold 15,000 people!

Athena the goddess of wisdom and peace, then dropped a seed into the soil and an olive tree instantly sprung from it. This tree was considered to be a symbol of peace and wisdom. The people of the city accepted this valuable gift by Athena and made her its guardian.

19 Did people bury their personal artefacts if they were destroyed ?

People are often known to treat their personal belongings as if they were living beings. However, of all the weird things that people have historically held a funeral for, the weirdest funeral was that held for an amputated leg. This state funeral was arranged for by Mexican General Antonio López de Santa Anna, the self-proclaimed 'Napoleon of the West'. In the 'Pastry War' against the French in 1838, Santa Anna was hit by a canon. The doctors were left with no option but to amputate his leg. Santa Anna buried this severed appendage at Veracruz hacienda. Once he became President in 1842, he dug up his leg and gave it a pompous and elaborate burial under a monument at the cemetery.

Santa Anna's leg

Born 1794

Died 1838

20 Why is the 1838 French-Mexican war called the 'Pastry War' ?

Believe it or not, but something as insignificant as an unpaid debt to a pastry chef, could spark off a war! This is exactly what happened in the year 1838, and the war that followed came to be known as the 'Pastry War'. After Mexico's independence from Spain, there was still a lot of violence prevalent amongst the civilians of the country. In this violence, the bakery of a French pastry chef, Remontel, was destroyed and he took the matter to the Mexican government, requesting some kind of compensation for his shop. When the Mexican government turned a deaf ear to his request, he approached his home country, the French king Louis Philippe.

The French were already upset about the pending debt that the Mexicans owed them and when they ignored the ultimatum by the French, the French Navy started taking over Mexican cities. When Mexican General Santa Anna got involved, a full-fledged war broke out, the 'Pastry War'.

21 How did we get the phrase 'spill the beans' ?

In ancient Greek, where democracy was invented, people used to vote using secret ballot. At the elections, there would be a huge jar and the people who cast their votes put a bean in this jar. A white bean meant 'Yes' and a black bean meant 'No'. The voters had access to beans of both colours. Once the elections were over, a minister would count the number of black and white beans, hence, declaring the decision of the majority of the people. This would happen only at the end of the elections, unless someone bumped into the jar and 'spilled the beans' so to say. Since then, 'spilling the beans' is a phrase used to mean giving away a secret.

22 How was the term 'Trojan Horse' coined ?

A 'Trojan horse' is a term used to represent someone or something that has a negative ulterior motive while seeming innocent.

In 1880 BCE, the Greeks were trying to take over the city of Troy, but the city was well protected with huge walls on all sides and only one huge gate that opened only for friends. In a sly and surprising strategy, the Greeks built a huge wooden horse and left it outside the gates of Troy. The people of Troy thought of it as a gift and brought it inside the gates of Troy. As soon as the horse was within the city, the Greek soldiers who were hiding inside the horse sprang out and took over the city. Such is the legend of the Trojan horse.

How did the Teddy bear get its name

Believe it or not, the Teddy bear got its name from the once US President, Theodore (Teddy) Roosevelt. In 1902, Roosevelt went hunting with Mississippi Governor Andrew H. Longino. When he couldn't track one himself, the hunting party spread out to capture a bear. A black bear was finally captured but a scuffle broke out between the hunting dogs and the bear, causing the bear to get injured. When Roosevelt arrived, the tired and injured bear was tied to a tree and he was asked to shoot it. However, Roosevelt did not feel that it was good sportsmanship and refused to shoot the bear. This event was covered by the newspapers as a cartoon depicting the bear as a cuddly and fluffy animal. To commemorate this event a penny-store owner got his wife to stitch a stuffed toy bear. These were sold in the market as 'Teddy's bear'.

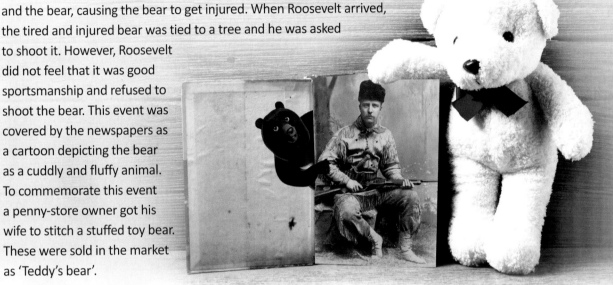

What is a petticoat duel

A duel was mostly fought between men in the event of a dispute. A man would challenge another to a battle of physical strength and skill. However, such a dispute could occur amongst women too and the duel they fought was called a petticoat duel. Whether this was because they fought in their petticoats or whether this was a name given to women's duels by men is yet to be known.

25 Who were Leonardo Da Vinci's parents?

Leonardo Da Vinci was born in 1452 in Tuscany, Italy. His father was Messer Piero Fruosino di Antonio da Vinci who was a well-known landlord in the region. His mother was a local peasant named Caterina. Both the parents lived separately and so he lived with his mother till he was 5 years old after which he went to live with his father.

It is said about Da Vinci that he was very close to his father and idolised him. He grieved deeply when his father passed away.

Although Da Vinci didn't meet his mother often, he did send her letters from time to time.

26 What is Pablo Picasso's full name?

Pablo Picasso's full name is Pablo Diego José Francisco de Paula Juan Nepomuceno María de los Remedios Cipriano de la Santísima Trinidad Martyr Patricio Clito Ruíz y Picasso. It consists of a total of 23 words!

Today, most often our full names consist of our first names, followed by our father's or husband's name (in case of women) and our last names. In other cases, the middle name is decided by our parents and is sometimes taken after one of our ancestors. However, in the olden days, the ancestor's names were passed on to their children and so many generations later, one of the successors would end up with a long name like Picasso's.

27 Why was Picasso accused of stealing the Mona Lisa ?

The truth of the matter is that for a brief period of time, the Mona Lisa was missing from her glass case. At the time that she went missing, there were about 150 guards protecting the entire Louvre that contained about 250,000 artefacts. This means that it was quite scarcely protected.

The person who stole the Mona Lisa was caught after trying to smuggle it back to Da Vinci's home country. His name was Peruggia.

However, during the course of the investigation, Pablo Picasso was arrested and there are many theories that indicate that Picasso could have planned the whole thing. To begin with, he was in France at the time of the robbery. Secondly, writer Guillaume Apollinaire who was a very good friend of Picasso was arrested for this robbery. Guillaume's employee had taken a statue to the editor of the Paris Journal to claim a prize they had declared for any information regarding the robbery at the Louvre. This statuette was stolen from the Louvre because of which Guillaume was arrested. Thirdly, Picasso had bought these very statuettes, which technically made him a buyer of stolen property. Fourthly, when called in for questioning by the police, Picasso refused to recognise him.

In spite of all these reasons and motives, Picasso and his friend were both released and Peruggia was arrested for the robbery. So was he really involved in stealing the Mona Lisa? We sure will never know.

28 — How did Beethoven become deaf ?

At that time, the medical authorities were not sure what caused Beethoven's deafness. However, over time as more research was carried out in the field, his deafness was attributed to consumption of lead over a long period of time. However, one wonders how Beethoven came to consume this lead. The answer is, wine. Beethoven was an avid wine drinker and used to drink a lot of wine, of the inexpensive variety. In the olden days, inexpensive wine was laced with lead to enhance its taste. This was illegal, but people drank it nevertheless. After Beethoven's mother passed away when he was 17, he took to drinking a lot causing his deafness.

29 — Why did Beethoven dip his head in cold water before composing music ?

Beethoven was a musical genius and like all other geniuses had too many things on his mind. He was known to dip his head in cold water before he composed his music. It is said that he also poured large amounts of water onto his hands, sometimes even wetting his clothes. He would then walk around in his room before finally sitting down to compose his music. There are various theories about this eccentricity of his. Some say that it was a way for him to refresh his mind. Like the way we splash water onto our face when we are sleepy or tired, Beethoven may have dipped his head in cold water to keep his mind alert and refresh it. Others say that it may have been a way to get his mind to think fast. Could it have been to break his other thought processes and allow him to focus on his work? Water has been known to refresh and stimulate. It sure helped him create beautiful music!

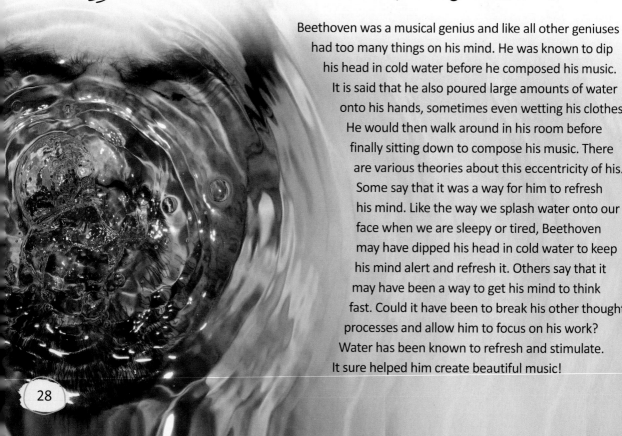

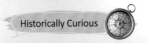

30 Who played the female roles in Shakespeare's plays back in the day ?

In the olden days, women were not allowed to step on the stage and display themselves to people. However, the plays written by Shakespeare had many female characters in it. So, young boys were hired to play the role of women. This means, Cordelia in *King Lear*, Portia in *The Merchant of Venice*, Lady Macbeth in *Macbeth*, Beatrice in *Much Ado About Nothing* and so on were all played by young boys.

Young boys were preferred for the roles because their facial hair was not fully developed, allowing them to look feminine using makeup. Besides, boys at that age are not muscular and could look petite and play a female role very convincingly. In addition to this, most of these boys were pre-pubescent and hence able to pitch their voice to sound like a woman.

Can you imagine the actor who played Portia in *The Merchant of Venice* was a boy playing a woman disguised as a man!

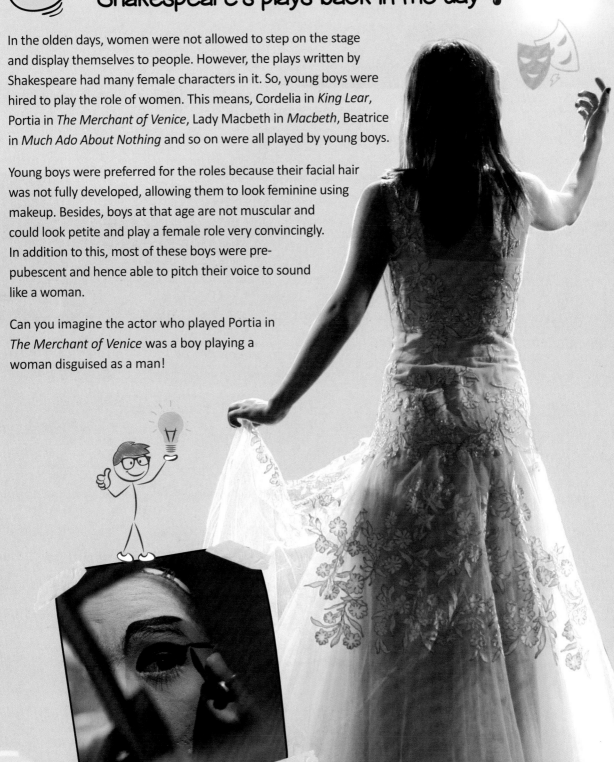

31 ❭ Why was Mozart suspected of being a dwarf ❓

Mozart had started playing and composing music at a very young age. He could play the piano very well at the age of 4 and by the age of 9, he was invited to play at the London auditorium. His performance was better than some of the experienced and aged performers of the time. He was so good at it that a lot of people found it unbelievable. When they investigated and found that there was no recording device that was playing the music, and that the 9-year-old was playing the music himself, they suspected that it must be a grown up in the body of a child. Imagine the child prodigy Mozart suspected of being a dwarf!

32 ❭ How did the term 'horsepower' come to be used ❓

The word 'horsepower' was coined by inventor James Watt. Many inventors had made improvements to the steam engine, but with James Watt's improvements, the word came greatly into use. He was the first person to measure the power generated by steam engines in terms of the number of horses required to generate the same amount of power. That is how the term horsepower came into use. We use this term even today when we say that a certain car has a certain amount of horsepower. One horsepower is equal to 745.7 watts.

A watt is a unit of power.
It was named after James Watt.

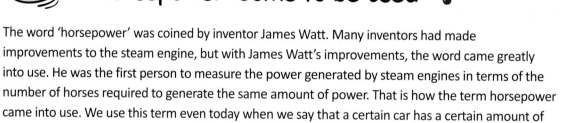

365 Amazing Questions and Answers

33 How did the Industrial Revolution get its name?

The term Industrial Revolution has two words. The first word 'Industrial' has a French origin and is drawn from the word, 'Industriel'. It could also have been drawn from the medieval Latin word, 'Industrialis' as they both mean 'activity, zeal or diligence'. These words were used to describe human characteristics, but over a period of time, it came to mean manufacturing commodities and machinery for large-scale production.

'Revolution' came from 'revolver' which meant to turn or roll back. It is this meaning of the word that came to be used metaphorically to mean 'a great change from the ordinary'.

34 Why is the Morse code also known as Victorian Internet?

The Morse code is a language of dots and dashes that is used to send messages from one telegraph to another. This language of dots and dashes was invented by Samuel Finley Breeze Morse. This equipment came to be used on such a large scale that all around the world, at least some parts of the country used the Morse code. This made it a (almost) global code language, not unlike the Internet that is available all over the world and can be accessed and updated globally from any corner of the Earth. Since the Morse code was active during the Victorian Era, it is now being referred to as the Victorian Internet.

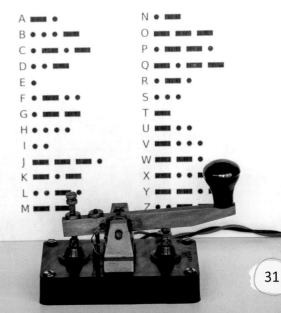

A ▄ •	N • ▄
B • • • ▄	O ▄ ▄ ▄
C • ▄ • ▄	P • ▄ ▄ •
D • • ▄	Q ▄ ▄ • ▄ ▄
E •	R • ▄ •
F • ▄ • •	S • • •
G • ▄ ▄	T ▄
H • • • •	U ▄ • •
I • •	V ▄ • • •
J ▄ ▄ ▄ •	W • ▄ •
K ▄ • ▄	X ▄ • • ▄
L • • • •	Y ▄ ▄ • •
M ▄ ▄	Z • • • ▄

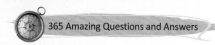
 35 Are pirates real

Pirates are very much real. They may seem like a fantastic bunch of people, but history is witness to many pirates who have looted and plundered valuables at sea. But do not fall for their swashbuckling, robin hoods of the sea image as you see in many movies and read in many books. Pirates were outlaws and terrorised the seven seas for many years. They stole from honest people and even killed many in order to acquire precious cargo transported by water. They were a constant crisis for many governments and people, who wanted to carry out peaceful trade through sea routes. You may not believe it, but there are many pirates in action even today. For example, pirates still make the rounds of the Gulf of Aden and hijack cargo ships that travel through these waters. As a precautionary measure, many countries send their naval forces to escort the cargo so that their valuables are protected from pirates.

36 Why do pirates say 'Arrr...' and 'matey' ?

Almost all the films we have seen about pirates show them having a guttural voice. They speak with heavy rolling Rs and using words like 'matey' and 'blimey'. However, this is historically incorrect. The image of the pirate that has been created today is all thanks to cinema. It all started when the first movie with a pirate character was made. The actor, Robert Newton, who was cast to play this role used a thick accent and rolled his Rs. Once he played this character, it became famous, and a pirate came to be recognised as someone who spoke that way. Add about 100 years of Hollywood to this, and we have the stereotypical image of a pirate in front of us today. However, don't be fooled, the real pirates of the olden days hardly spoke the way we expected them to.

37 Was Julius Caesar really kidnapped by pirates ?

History speaks of the kidnapping of Julius Caesar at the age of 25 by Sicilian pirates. One would think that something like this would traumatise an individual for the rest of their life, but not Caesar. The Roman General, however, didn't stay onboard the ship as a victim but rather treated his kidnappers as his comrades. He wrote and shared poetry with them and practiced his speeches with them. Not only that, the pirates had asked for a ransom of 20 talents of silver for the safe return of Julius Caesar but Caesar insisted that they asked for 50 which is about 1550 kg of silver! It all seemed quite amicable but as soon as the ransom was paid and Caesar was let go, he put together a small attacking fleet of ships and attacked the pirates, and acquiring the 50 talents of silver as well.

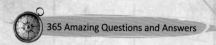
38 Why did pirates wear an eye patch and have wooden limbs

No matter how adventurous and amazing a pirate's life may seem, it is a life full of perils and hardships. If you haven't already, try taking a boat ride. The first few minutes are fun, but soon the rocking of the boat will bring about motion sickness. Now imagine how magnified the effects of this sickness would be when one is onboard a ship in the middle of the ocean and weathering a storm. Even regular sailors could end up emptying the contents of their stomach. Besides, the roll and the pitch of the ship makes it difficult to find ones bearings. Not only pirates, but generally anybody who lives onboard a ship without proper safety measures, ends up in a lot of accidents. In days gone by, pirates had to brave storms and combats with no safety measures in place. They often ended up losing their eyes and limbs. And hence they were invariably depicted with eye patches and wooden prosthetics.

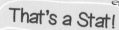

That's a Stat!

Pirates might seem historical, however, there have been 246 pirate attacks worldwide from 2009 to 2015.

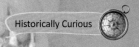

39 How did the Olympic games begin?

The Olympic Games began as a set of competitions held on the plains of Olympia, by the Greeks to please the gods who, according to Greek mythology, lived on Mount Olympus. The Games were said to have been started by the Greek god Herakles in honour of Zeus when he defeated Cronus as they fought for the throne of gods. Each game represented one of the religious festivals celebrated by the worshippers of Zeus. However, the Olympic Games were not meant only for religious purposes. They were played even to display the physical strength and accuracy of the youth of Greece. At the end of the Games, the winners were announced along with the name of their father and the name of the city they came from. More and more people played and participated in these games which ended up bringing people together in society. People from far and wide came to compete and fight for their chance to fame. This ritual was banned for a period of time by the church as the Greek gods were considered pagan. However, they started off again and we continue to hold them once every four years.

40 Did duels really happen in the olden days ?

Yes, duels are as true as the people who fought them. And one of the most interesting duels fought was by the famous novelist and writer of *The Man in the Iron Mask*, Alexandre Dumas. So what made this young writer forego his pen and reach for a sword? It seems that one of the soldiers at a local café made fun of his coat and boots. A proper French man that Dumas was, he challenged the soldier to a duel. Now it was snowing heavily outside, but they still managed to find a spot to match their fencing skills. Dumas was asked to take off not only his coat but his shirt as well for which he had to take off his suspenders. With the thing holding up his pants out of the way, they fell down to the floor, drawing laughter from onlookers. Dumas managed to secure his pants with the suspenders again and started the duel. He had the last laugh as he won the duel.

Day-to-Day Wonders

We live in a wonderful world but life hardly gives us the chance to stop and ponder. There are so many things around us that we take for granted. Have you ever wondered why somethings happen? The answers are as amazing as the world we live in.

41 Why are the buttons on the opposite sides in men's and women's shirts?

The most commonly believed reason for men and women having buttons on the opposite side of the shirt is that in the olden days, men usually dressed themselves and hence it was convenient to have buttons on the right. The women, however, wore such elaborate clothing that they had to be dressed by their maids and so the buttons were made convenient for someone else to put on the wearer of the shirt.

However, a more practical reason is that women with babies hold the child with their left hand to keep their right hand free. So, while nursing the baby, the mother could unbutton her shirt with the right hand if the buttons are on the left panel.

42 How did the word SPAM originate?

Few people know that the word has its origins in Monty Python's *Flying Circus* skit, way back in the 1970s, where a waitress in a restaurant kept saying SPAM while reading the menu. Here, SPAM stood for a brand of meat. That is when a group of Vikings at the corner table started to sing a song repeating the same word. They kept singing it till nobody in the restaurant could hear each other. The Vikings were finally asked to keep quiet. This is how SPAM came to be known as an annoying message that keeps repeating itself and interrupts you.

43 Why do we park in driveways and drive on parkways?

We park our cars on driveways because in olden days, driveways used to be much longer than what we have now. So someone would have to drive their car to the house on the driveway and then park their car. That is how we ended up parking in our one-car long driveways.

Driving on parkways is quite simple to explain considering that the word 'Park' has two meanings. A park also means a place of scenic beauty that is adorned by trees and plants that people visit for leisure. In olden days, a parkway would be a scenic road going through a park. Hence, the term driving down the parkway stuck.

44 Why are the windows of an airplane not always aligned with the seats ?

When you sit in an airplane, you will notice that the windows don't all align with the seats of the airplane. Sometimes, the window might even be between two seats which doesn't seem very practical. The reason for this is that the manufacturers design the seats aligned with the windows, however, to be more efficient or to be able to seat more people, the buyers of the aircraft shift the seats on the plane causing the alignment to get disturbed.

Most of the seats on the plane are attached on a track. Also, variable tracks are available so that the seats may be easily shifted, removed or replaced. This is designed in a flexible way as due to various technical reasons, the aircraft owner may want to move around the seats in the plane. Sometimes, the aircraft owner may move entire rows of seats in order to accommodate additional necessary elements on the plane. This is why you will notice that the aisle space in some planes may be more or less than others. This flexibility allows the owners to make optimum use of the space in the aircraft. And that is why, you need to stretch in order to look out of the windows on a flight.

45 Why are apples gifted to teachers ?

Around the 19th century, teachers were funded by the people of the town. Families would come together and provide for the daily basic needs of the teacher. Soon, however, the government took over this responsibility but families still continued to make contributions to the teachers every now and then. This was to show that they appreciated what the teachers taught their children as well as a way to get in the good books of the teacher. Also, apples were used to make cider which was considered safer than water. Apples made a good snack as well as a good drink for the teacher.

46 Why are the Oscar Awards called thus ?

Oscar Awards are one of the most prestigious and most coveted awards known in the entertainment industry. The actual name of the award is Academy Awards. Oscar is the nickname of the statuette that is presented to the winners of the award. The statuette is that of a knight standing on a reel of film holding a crusader's sword and is made in a pewter-like alloy that is then coated with copper, nickel, silver and finally, pure gold. How the statuette got the name is not very well-known, however, the most popular story is that the Academy librarian Margaret Hick had said that the statue looked like her Uncle Oscar on seeing it for the first time.

(47) Why do Don't Walk signs drop the apostrophe ?

One reason, and a far-fetched one at that, is that it makes the word easier to read and understand. Words with apostrophes are said to be more confusing to read as opposed to words without them. As it is important for the message of the signal to get across as soon as possible, the sign was left without an apostrophe.

Another reason is that it was to match the spacing of the words when the word 'Don't' appeared above the word 'Walk'. However, this too doesn't seem to justify the grammatical incorrectness of the phrase.

A third reason is that since the signs were made of neon, they were fashioned out of a single neon tube that was bent to make the word, and it was difficult to add the apostrophe. This technical difficulty could be the reason why the apostrophe was simply dropped out of the word as it did not change the meaning of the word, yet made it simpler to read.

48 Why are there 8 hours in a working day ?

Previously, factory workers worked 24X7, 16-18 hours a day. However, the productivity suffered. That is when, Robert Owen proposed his campaign, '8 hours labour, 8 hours recreation, 8 hours rest'.

Ford Motors, not only took up the 8 hour working day standard but also doubled the workers' wages, resulting in a huge improvement in worker efficiency and within a couple of years, their productivity doubled.

Following this example, other companies reduced their working hours as well, and hence, today we have an 8-hour working day.

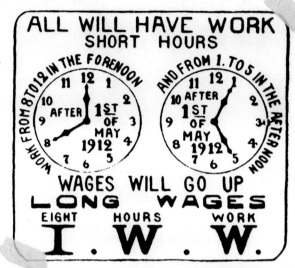

ALL WILL HAVE WORK
SHORT HOURS
WORK FROM 8 TO 12 IN THE FORENOON
AFTER 1ST OF MAY 1912
AND FROM 1. TO 5 IN THE AFTERNOON
AFTER 1ST OF MAY 1912
WAGES WILL GO UP
LONG WAGES
EIGHT HOURS WORK
I . W . W .

49 Why do some fans have three blades and other have four ?

Fans that have three blades are faster than those with four. In that case, why wouldn't everyone use three-bladed fans? The answer to this question depends upon the geographical locations in which the fans are used. Usually, you will find three-bladed fans in countries where fans are used on their own for ventilation and cooling, namely India. Here, the objective is to increase the force of the air in order to cool the room. However, in other countries where fans are used to supplement the air conditioning, namely the US, four-bladed fans are used. This is because the objective is not to increase the force of the air but to simply move it as much as possible. That is why different countries have three or four blades on their fans.

50 Why does the English language have silent letters?

Don't you think that English is a confusing language? And one of the things that adds to the confusion is the existence of words with silent letters. What is the point of adding letters that won't even get pronounced to the spelling of a word? Well, as literature would have it, they do have a reason. Firstly, silent letters can indicate the origin, the etymology of the word. English is a language that has been inspired, and it has adopted words from various other languages. The use of silent words allows you to understand the history of the word. For example, we know that 'Rendezvous' is a French word because of the way it is pronounced.

Secondly, silent letters indicate the difference between homophonic words when they are written. For example, write and rite sound exactly the same, but thanks to the silent W, you can tell the difference between the two words when they are written.

Finally, if we were to write all the words we know the way we pronounce them, we would have to add many more letters to the alphabet. Not to mention that we would end up spelling our words differently from everyone else.

So, as you see, silent letters are not unnecessary in a word. They are there for a reason and are indeed quite helpful.

Don't miss it!

the most awaited
MOVIE
of the year

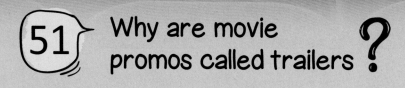

51 Why are movie promos called trailers ?

Today, movie producers have many ways of advertising their movies. We see promos on TV. Often the music is released a couple of months before the movie itself adding to the excitement and the fandom of the movie. However, you may have gone to a theatre to watch a movie and seen many promos played before the movie as well. For a very long time, this was the only way to advertise a new and upcoming movie. This was the time when TV was not yet a household object. They used to be called and continue to be called trailers. The reason people called them trailers is because in the earlier days, these promos were often seen at the end of the movie. Since they trailed on after the movie, they came to be known as trailers. However, soon the audience started leaving the theatre as soon as the movie ended, and there was no one left to watch the trailers. The distributors found that their movies were not being advertised due to this, but they were also quick to notice that the audience ensured that they were in the theatre before the movie started. They, therefore, decided to make use of the few minutes before the movie to advertise the upcoming movies. This is how trailers came to be shown before the movies but continued to be called trailers.

52 Does the blue part of an eraser really erase ink ?

We all have seen double-sided erasers that are blue at one end and red at the other. The red end erases pencil writing, and the myth was that the blue end erased ink. But does it really? The answer is no. The red side is soft and can get rid of pencil marks on normal paper. However, because it is soft, it does not have enough traction on heavy paper or thick paper. For this, we have the gritty blue side that can create enough friction on this paper to get rid of the pencil marks. Now that you know what the blue end is for, don't go trying to erase pen marks, or you might end up with a few holes in your books.

That's a Stat!

27,000 trees are cut daily all over the world to create toilet paper. About 45 kg of toilet paper can be made out of a single tree.

53 Why do you get an extra piece of fabric and buttons attached to new clothes ?

When you buy branded clothes, more often than not, they come with extra buttons as well as a small patch of fabric that the clothing item is made up of. You might wonder what this small piece of fabric could do, especially since it is too small even for patch-up jobs. The true purpose of this piece of fabric is to test your washing detergent on. This piece can be washed in your washing machine and tested to see how it affects the quality of the material. Some new items of clothing lose colour on washing. So, if you test the piece of cloth in water, you know this and will refrain from washing the item with your whites, unless you prefer pastel-coloured socks or underwear!

54 Why is there a little hole in a padlock?

A typical padlock, is a metal item ranging from a few centimetres to half a foot in size that can be used to lock doors, gates and practically anything with a latch. However, some padlocks have a tiny hole at the bottom, next to the keyhole. This seemingly insignificant orifice also has a purpose. The first use is that of drainage. When it rains, water can trickle into the lock, and if it stays inside, it may rust causing the lock to get jammed and eventually be rendered useless. So the tiny hole forms an outlet for it, helping to keep the lock dry and not get rusted. The second use is for oiling. The mechanism of a lock needs oiling from time to time for its smooth use. Oil can be poured through this tiny hole to keep the lock well lubricated and rust-free.

However, do not be too concerned if your lock does not have this hole. It may be because your lock doesn't need one as it is made of rust-free metal.

55 Why is there a little hole in the pen cap ?

Let's take another look at your pen. Look closely at the cap this time. You will find another hole. It has been put there with a purpose. The first reason is practical. For the pen cap to stay on the pen, there will need to be some air in the cap that gets released as it is pushed onto the pen. The hole in the cap allows this. It also reduces undue pressure on the nib. The second and more important reason, is to avoid a crisis if the cap is ever swallowed by anyone, since it is so small. In such cases, the cap can get lodged in the trachea and without the hole in the cap, it would cause the person to choke. However, with the hole, the air can still reach the lungs. Believe it or not, but this tiny hole has saved several lives till date.

56 Why is there a little hole at the side of your pen ?

If you take a closer look at the body of your pen, you will notice a small hole in it. Ever wondered why this hole exists? It does not serve any aesthetic purpose. The reason for this hole is to regulate the pressure of the ink inside the refill. Without this hole, the body of the pen would be packed once the back end was sealed. The ink would not have any air to push it forward, causing the ink to jam and making the pen useless. With the help of the hole, the air enters the refill causing the ink in it to flow out through the nib.

This hole also keeps the pen from exploding or leaking in high pressure places like in an airplane or on mountains.

57 Why is there a dimple at the bottom of wine bottles?

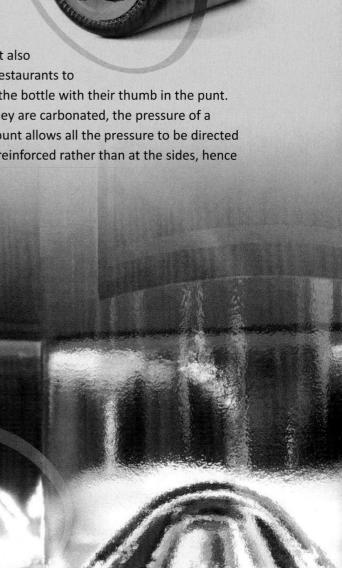

If you've had the chance to notice the bottom of wine bottles, you might have seen that it has a dimple. It looks like the bottom of the bottle has been pushed inwards. This indent is called a punt. The punts exist in wine bottles because in olden days, these bottles were created by glass blowers. They manually blew through pipes with blobs of molten glass at the other end. While blowing these bottles, the punt enabled the bottles to stand upright by making them bottom-heavy. It also allows sommeliers, the wine experts at fancy restaurants to pour wine or champagne in a glass by holding the bottle with their thumb in the punt. The third use is for sparkling wines. Because they are carbonated, the pressure of a sealed bottle may increase if it is shaken. The punt allows all the pressure to be directed at the bottom of the bottle where it has been reinforced rather than at the sides, hence preventing it from exploding.

58 What is the small cylinder at the end of a laptop charger ?

Some things just exist, and we don't even question them until they are pointed out to us. We all have seen a laptop charger at some point or the other and have seen this little cylindrical bump at the end of it as well. But do you know what it is there for? Well, the bump is called a ferrite bead. Named thus, because the bead is entirely made of ferrite. This is a material that blocks electrical interference. When charging your laptop, you don't want other electrical appliances to mess up the flow of electricity into your laptop. And that is exactly what this bead does, extending the life of your laptop in the process. If your laptop charger does not have one, you can easily get them in the market.

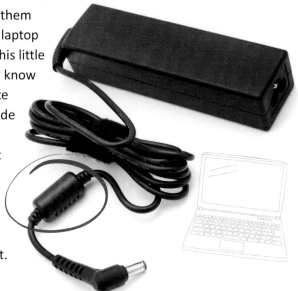

59 Why is there a hole in airplane windows ?

If you have ever taken a flight, then you know the hole that we are talking about. This is the tiny hole at the bottom centre of the round airplane windows. This tiny hole regulates the pressure of the glass. The window is actually made up of two sheets of glass. The outer sheet is of layers of high-quality fibreglass as it has to withstand the outer pressure. The inner sheet is cheaper and made of Plexiglas as it doesn't have to withstand a lot of pressure. However, the two sheets of glass next to each other, exposed to varying amounts of pressure can cause it to shatter. This is why we have the tiny hole. The tiny hole also keeps the pressure outside the airplane away from the windows.

60 How did the term Box-Office come to be ?

The term Box-Office is used today to denote the amount of money a particular movie made in the market. If the movie earns a lot, it is a Box-Office hit, if not, then a flop. However, this term Box-Office was coined a long time ago during the Elizabethan era when there were theatres and people paid money to watch plays. As it happens even today, before you entered the theatre, which was usually an open ground, you had to buy a ticket from an office at the entrance of the theatre. All the money collected from selling the tickets would then be kept in a box and locked up in the office. And that is how we get the term, Box-Office.

61 Why are there pocket rivets on your jeans ?

Levis Strauss invented jeans for gold collectors. Initially, trousers were made of canvas but Strauss started using a softer version which was much more comfortable and cheaper, i.e., denim. However, this material was also weak at the seams, especially since the gold collectors put nuggets of gold in their pockets and they would rip because of the weight. Later, in 1872, Jacob Davis a tailor, started using bits of metal to secure the seams of the pockets. That is why, today, you have rivets at the corners of your jeans pockets. It is of no use these days, but they sure add to the look of your jeans.

Why is there a groove between the nose and the upper lip ?

62

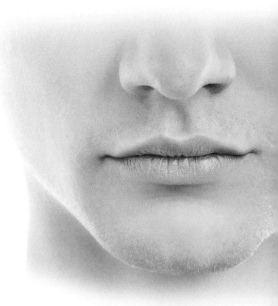

We all have it and caress it carelessly when we are in deep thought. But look at a mirror and you won't even think twice about it. This is the small groove running from the bottom of your nose to the top of the lip. Why do we have it? Well, this piece of skin called philtrum isn't of any practical use but is key to how faces are formed when the embryo is still developing in the mother's womb. This groove is where the main components of your face come together while your body is still being formed before your birth. It happens in the second and third month of pregnancy, and if this process is interrupted due to any complications, then the baby is born with a hair-lip.

Where are croissants from ?

63

Croissants are a soft and fluffy form of puff pastry that one enjoys mostly with tea. Although it can be classified as bread, it is much more than that and has an almost melt-in-the-mouth texture. This bread is made by rolling out a sheet of dough, cutting it into thin strips and then rolling it up and baking it. The air trapped when the dough is rolled makes the pastry soft and fluffy, especially when eaten freshly baked. The name of the pastry croissant is a French word meaning 'crescent', which describes the shape of the pastry. However, in spite of its name, croissants do not hail from France. They are actually created in Vienna in Austria. So now you know that croissants were Austrian.

(64) How did the Barbie doll come to be named so ?

Barbie is a household name for families with children. If you haven't played with one, you may have seen your sister or friends play with one. The Barbie doll is classically a tall, slender doll with a cascading waterfall of blonde hair, and a range of outfits available in the market to deck her up with. However, very few people know that Barbie has a last name too. Her full name is Barbara Millicent Roberts. She has been named after the daughter of the founders of Mattel, the toy company that produces Barbie dolls. Ruth Handler realised that her daughter was more interested in playing with dolls of adult women made out of paper rather than her usual baby dolls. This resulted in the mass production of Barbie that kids adore these days.

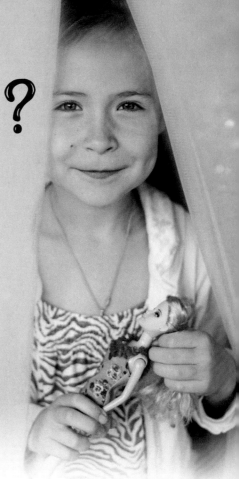

(65) Why do mosquitoes bite some people more than others ?

Haven't you ever seen those pesky little mosquitoes buzzing your way in a crowded room and wondered, 'Why me?' It may not have been you, they may even fly towards another individual and this again would make you curious. 'Why him?' We often make fun of the fact by saying, 'May be my blood is sweeter than yours.' But that is quite far from the truth. As opposed to flies, who are attracted to sweet food stuff, mosquitoes are guided by the scent of sweat. So, the next time you see mosquitoes attracted to you, quit feeling boastful and get yourself an overdue hot shower.

66 How was chocolate milk invented?

Chocolate drinks were developed in Jamaica as a welcome drink. However, chocolate was used ages before that. Believe it or not, chocolate was administered as medicine to people. The medical authorities of the Mesoamerican culture tested chocolate and found it to have cold and dry properties, which means it could be used to treat hot and wet health conditions like fever and mucous. It was only later on that it came to be used more for its taste and to cover the bitter taste of other medicines. Many years on, an Irish botanist Sir Hans Sloane added milk to the chocolate drink offered to him by the Jamaicans and created the chocolate milk that we love so much.

67 What does the little arrow next to the petrol symbol on the petrol gauge indicate?

An adult driving a car will tell you the use of most of the dials in a car, but have you observed a little icon showing a petrol pump on the petrol gauge? This symbol has a little arrow next to it. In some cars this arrow points left and in others, it points right. The purpose of this arrow is known to a few and is very simple as well as helpful. It simply indicates which side of the car has the petrol tank. Usually, you would know this if you owned a car. However, if the car is new, borrowed or rented, the driver would have to stick his head out of the window to know the side that has the petrol tank. This little arrow makes it immediately apparent, and the driver can decide the side to park the car when refuelling.

68 How to open an Internet tab that you have just closed on the computer ?

How often have you hit the 'X' on your computer before completing your work? There are times when we end up closing tabs prematurely and then wondering what website that was. So this is what you can do. If you have just closed the tab, then using your keyboard press Control/Command+Shift+T. This will immediately open the Internet tab that you closed no matter what browser you are using. If you want to access a webpage you visited yesterday or a few days ago, then go into your browser history and look up the page. Remember this keyboard shortcut, it will come in handy the next time you click 'Close' without thinking.

69 Do we have only five senses ?

You must have learnt in school that we have five senses. We do have five sensory organs, but our senses exceed these. The five basic senses are sight, smell, taste, hearing and touch. But we also feel the passage of time. It may be relative and may pass quickly for some and slow for others, but we do feel it. There is also temperature and pressure. This is not the same as touch as we feel these even without touching. On the other hand, we also feel hunger and thirst. What about maintaining balance? If you are standing on one foot or riding a bicycle, your body adjusts itself to maintain its equilibrium. So, yes, we definitely have more than five senses.

70 What is the dot over the letter 'i' called ?

The English letters of the alphabet were not always the way they are today. They have gone through many variations and versions before they ended up as 26 letters with a capital and small script. Also, since English borrows parts of its script from other languages, we see that many components of the alphabets are shared. A good example of this is the tittle. The dot over the letter 'i' as well as 'j' is called a tittle and is seen in many other scripts including Arabic and Hebrew. In the English alphabet, the tittle is simply a way to complete the letter of the alphabet, however, in other languages, the alphabets include an 'i' with the tittle and an 'i' without the tittle which is significant to the meaning of the word.

71 Do sunflowers really clean up nuclear waste ?

Our planet has seen a number of nuclear disasters. Due to this, we need a force strong enough to clean up the nuclear waste left in the soil to avoid radioactive exposure. And what do you think can fight nuclear power? The answer is nature. Vast fields of sunflower plants have been planted along the areas affected by nuclear disasters with the hope that it will dispose of the nuclear waste. Sunflowers are known as hyper accumulators. They have strong roots that absorb metals and radiation from the soil and accumulate it in their stem and leaves. Admitted that it is a slow process and the efficiency of all the variants of the sunflower family cannot be vouched for, but it is a beginning.

72 What is the easiest way to get rid of a splinter ?

A cut can be cleaned and bandaged, but a splinter is a foreign body in your skin and your body lets you know it's there by generating pain. Usually, you would use tweezers and a magnifying glass, but there is an easier way. Wash your hands with soap and dry them completely. Apply white school glue to the splinter and leave it to dry. It has to dry completely so give it about half an hour. Once dry, slowly peel the glue in the direction that the splinter entered your skin. Check the glue to see if the splinter has been removed. If not, try the tweezer method. However, 4 out of 5 times, the splinter can be removed in this way. Do not use instant glue for this.

73 Are bank notes made of paper or cotton ?

There is a lot of contradictory information available on the Internet about whether bank notes are made from paper or cotton. The truth of the matter is that both the answers are partially correct. Technically, banknotes are made from paper. But the question is, what is that paper made from? Normal paper is made from wood pulp and contains cellulose. So does the pulp that is used to create bank notes. However, money-pulp also includes a high percentage of cotton and linen. It is estimated that money-paper is 75 per cent cotton and 25 per cent linen. This gives the paper durability. This is also the reason why the paper doesn't tear very easily and can be distinguished from fakes as it doesn't glow under black light like normal paper does.

74 Why do we like chocolate so much ?

There are some people in the world whose first-aid kit would include a bar of chocolate. Other than the fact that it tastes very good, it also ends up making you feel better. There is a reason why women are shown eating chocolate when sad in TV shows and movies. But what is the reason behind chocolate affecting us in such a way? To begin with, a lot of chocolates contain sugar that 'wakes us up', making us feel more alert and refreshed. However, even if you keep the sugar aside, plain chocolate is known to contain a chemical called 'anandamide' that also exists in our brain naturally. This chemical is what makes us feel happy. When the chocolate is being produced this anandamide breaks down but it manages to enhance the effects of the natural anandamide in our brain making us feel positive and cheerful almost four times longer than usual. Now you can scientifically explain your chocolate cravings.

75 Why does a raisin dropped in soda keep bouncing up and down ?

Use this trick to entertain your friends the next time they are over. Take a glass of clear soda and add a raisin to it. The raisin will sink to the bottom of the glass, then it will rise back up to the surface. Once at the surface, the raisin will sink back to the bottom of the glass. It is fun to watch, but why does it happen? The reason is the carbon dioxide in the drink. Because a raisin is shrivelled up, the carbon dioxide bubbles can cling to its many wrinkles. Once the bubbles have attached to the raisin, it rises to the surface. At the surface, the carbon dioxide bubbles pop and dissolve in the air. The raisin becomes heavy again and sinks to the bottom. This continues till all the carbon dioxide in the soda runs out.

76 Why are there no clocks in the Las Vegas casinos ?

You might have read about this or seen it in a movie, how casinos at Las Vegas have no clocks. What you perhaps may not have observed is that they also do not have any windows. Another thing you may not know is that it is not only the Las Vegas casinos, but most of the casinos in the world do not have windows or clocks. The reason is simple, so that people gambling inside the casino lose track of time and end up spending more time than expected. There are stories of people who kept gambling for days on end until they lost all their money. So the lack of a time-telling device on the decorated walls of these gambling houses, is not due to oversight or forgetfulness, but due to a cunning scheme to trap outsiders and ensure that they continue gambling for as long as possible.

77 How do you fix glasses whose screws keep coming loose ?

A good pair of glasses lasts long if taken good care of. But sometimes their screws may come loose. If they have lost their thread, no matter how much you tighten them, they will fall off. There is a very simple solution for this. You might have clear nail paint of your own or one of your family members is bound to own one. If neither is available then you have an excuse to go shopping. After tightening the screws of your glasses as best as you can, add a touch of clear nail paint to it and let it dry overnight. Once dried and hardened, the screw will not come loose again allowing you to use it for as many more years as you like.

78 Does the Guinness Book of World Records itself hold any records ?

The Guinness Book of World Records maintains a record of all the world records held by people all over the globe. However, this book of records also holds a record of its own. The record it holds is in the most copies of a book stolen from a public library. A person who has read the Guinness Book of World Records will know that it is an interesting book full of weird facts and figures, so it seems plausible that not many people return the book once checked out, or some may even sneak one out while the librarian isn't looking. This makes it the book with most copies stolen from public libraries.

WORLD RECORD

That's a Stat!

A survey by the Bible society suggests that about 5 billion copies of the Bible have been printed till date.

79 How do we multitask ?

Multitasking refers to the ability to do multiple tasks at the same time, but how do we do it? To begin with, multitasking is a myth. The brain cannot concentrate on two things at once. When a person multitasks, they simply turn off their concentration from one task and move it to another. Multitasking is nothing but flitting your attention between multiple tasks at hand, giving your full attention to one task at a time. So if you feel like multitasking isn't your cup of tea, give it a shot. Practice it for some time, and you will get the hang of it. It is simply a matter of mind over matter.

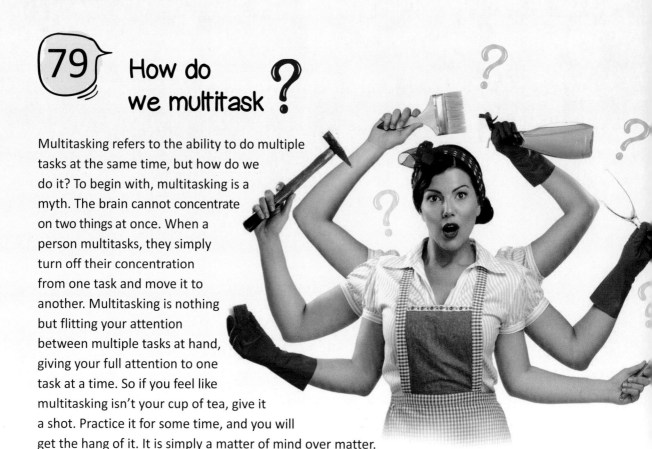

80 What is Eigengrau ?

At one point or another, each one of us has tried to imagine a new colour but failed. However, scientists have named a new colour. This is the colour that we see when it is completely dark. Try it. Turn the lights out in the room at night, and try to see what colour is in front of your eyes. Although the phrase is 'pitch black' the colour that you are seeing is not black, but Eigengrau. If we try to describe this colour then it is majorly black with small amounts of blue and red. Also, Eigengrau is a little bit lighter than black.

#000000 BLACK

#16161D EIGENGRAU

Interesting Medicines

81 Why do people suffering from cancer lose hair ?

We see a lot of cancer awareness campaigns, and the people who represent these, or those undergoing treatment, are usually without hair. It makes you wonder what the abnormal mutation of the cells in your body has to do with your hair follicles. However, the fact is that cancer patients don't lose their hair because of cancer, but because of its treatment, specifically, the chemotherapy. This therapy gets rid of all dividing cells. Cancer as you know is caused due to tumour forming, abnormally dividing cells. However, the normal dividing cells that are present in the lining of our scalp and cause our hair to grow, are also destroyed in chemotherapy. That is why most cancer patients lose their hair.

82 What is the Powder of Sympathy ?

Many centuries ago, magic was a part of medication. Around the 17th century, the Powder of Sympathy came into existence. It consisted of soil, earthworms, iron oxide and body parts of animals and sometimes, of humans. This was meant to cure rapier wounds. A rapier is a thin sword, not unlike a fencing sword, but one that is mostly used for thrusting. So if a man was injured by this sword, the Powder of Sympathy would be applied, not to the wound, but to the sword itself! Now, do you understand why it was called the Powder of Sympathy?

83 Did they do a urine test in olden days ?

Today if you are sick and your General Practitioner cannot tell what is wrong with you, they refer you for a blood and urine test. These two fluids can reveal what is wrong with your body. It seems that the doctors of Medieval Europe did have an idea of this, because they asked their patients to submit a sample of urine. However, their testing was basically to observe the colour and consistency of the liquid after which they often arrived at a diagnosis based on how the urine smelled, looked or even tasted (Yuck!).

84 What does snake oil mean ?

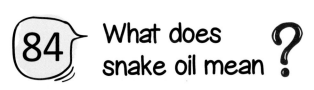

Snake oil is a term that is used to describe medication that is of no value. It also describes any suggested solution that offers no help for the problem at hand. However, before becoming a term with negative connotations, snake oil was really used for medical purposes. Traditionally, the Chinese have been using it as a way to relieve pain and continue to use it today.

They rubbed it into their joints when they began to hurt from a hard day's work. Scientifically, it has been shown that snake oil is rich in Omega-3 fatty acids that fight inflammation.

85 How was mouldy bread a part of the medication in olden days ?

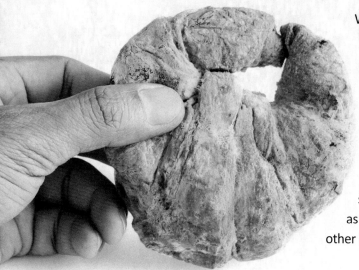

When you think of health, the last thing that comes to your mind is mouldy bread, unless you are thinking of things to avoid to stay healthy. In that case, why would someone use mouldy bread as a part of medication? The basic reason that we avoid it is because of the fungus and bacteria that grows on it. However, in olden days, this mouldy bread was sometimes used to disinfect wounds. Don't be so shocked. It was later found that this was useful as some forms of bacteria hampered the growth of other harmful organisms, almost like penicillin.

86 What was Vin Mariani ?

Vin Mariani literally means Wine of Mariani. Angelo Mariani was an Italian chemist who came up with this medication in 1863. It consisted of red wine that included components of coca leaves. This medication became so popular at the time that it was administered even to the Pope and royalty of many countries. The popularity of this medicine, however, was less due to its healing properties and more due to its addictive properties, as the harmful drug cocaine comes from the very same coca leaves that were used in this medication. This concoction, minus its harmful components, became the inspiration for Cola drinks.

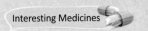

 87 Did aroma therapy exist in the middle ages **?**

The middle ages were a very curious time in the study of medicine. The raging medical belief back then was fighting fire with fire. The disease was treated by administering the symptoms of the same disease to the patient. For example, the disease called Black Death was caused because of deadly vapours, and according to the theory, the way to treat these was with the help of vapours. In such a case, people kept goats in the house for their foul smell. Others went a step beyond and gathered flatulence in a jar. So, as you see, there was indeed 'aroma' therapy in the olden days. However, it came with a medieval twist!

88 What were the alternative methods used to relieve a toothache?

Have any of you suffered from a toothache? The pain is unbearable. It can bring even the mightiest to their knees. There are many homemade remedies to get rid of a toothache, namely, rubbing salt on it or using eucalyptus oil. However, the weirdest and the most disgusting cure ever thought of, was by the ancient Egyptians. Believe it or not, they used a paste which, along with many other ingredients, also consisted of the body parts of a mouse! This ointment was then rubbed on to the offending tooth. There is no explanation as to why they thought that it would help, and scientists haven't been able to find a practical reason for this either. What would you do if you had to choose between a toothache and mouse paste in your mouth? Back then, a lot of people probably bore their toothache in silence.

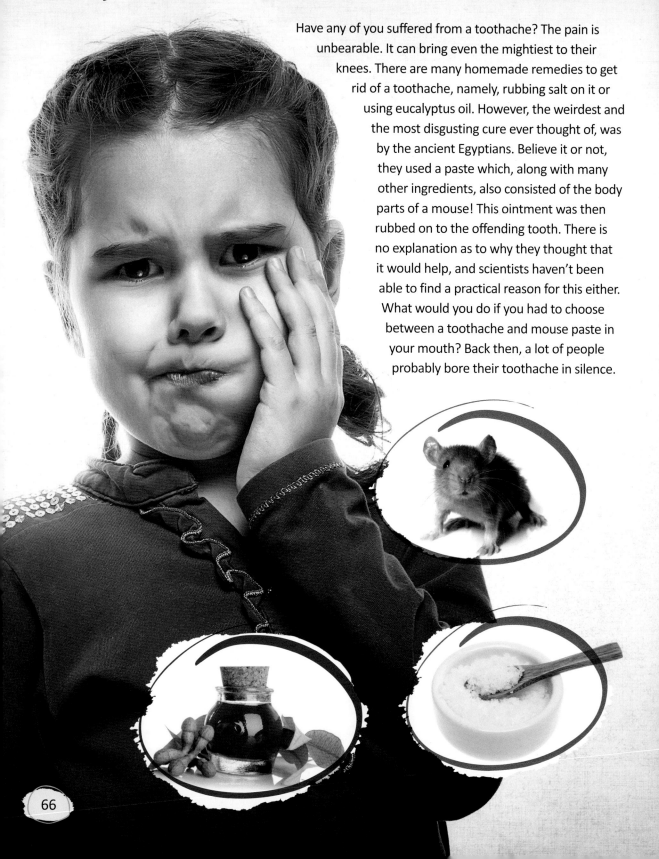

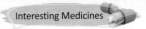

 89 What is the weirdest known method to cure stuttering ?

Some doctors of the 18th and 19th century, took the term 'cutting your losses' very seriously. Today, if your appendix is giving you trouble, it is surgically removed. If your tonsils are swollen, they could be treated or removed. But what if you stuttered? There was no speech therapy in olden days, and the doctors thought it was a good idea to reduce the length of their patient's tongue!

Hemiglossectomy is an operation in which a part of the tongue is surgically removed. It is done today to treat oral cancer and that too under heavy sedation. It might have been a better idea back then to pretend to be mute instead!

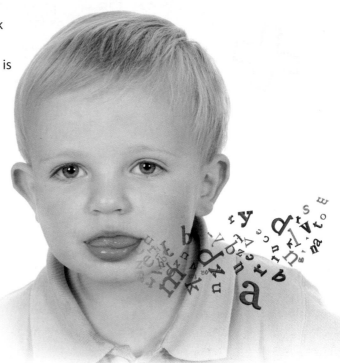

 90 Before X-ray machines and blood tests, how did doctors diagnose a patient ?

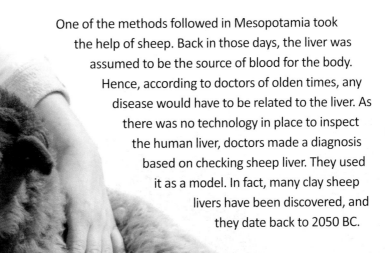

One of the methods followed in Mesopotamia took the help of sheep. Back in those days, the liver was assumed to be the source of blood for the body. Hence, according to doctors of olden times, any disease would have to be related to the liver. As there was no technology in place to inspect the human liver, doctors made a diagnosis based on checking sheep liver. They used it as a model. In fact, many clay sheep livers have been discovered, and they date back to 2050 BC.

91 What is phlebotomy ?

Phlebotomy is the process by which medical professionals remove blood from the body. This practice was largely followed in medieval times, when doctors believed that the cure to most diseases was to drain the infected blood from the body. Many crass and painful methods were used at that time. Often, the person who applied the incision to carry out the bloodletting (another word for phlebotomy) was the local barber. This is why the post outside a barber's shop also has a red stripe. Today, phlebotomy is practised on a very small scale and mostly to treat hemochromatosis where a person has too much iron in his blood.

92 How were leeches used in the field of medicine ?

Leeches are slug like parasites with teeth and a sucker like mouth, which they use to attach themselves to their host and suck blood. Healers of medieval Europe used this characteristic of leeches to help relieve pressure on body parts with internal bleeding. The leeches would suck out all the extra or even infected blood. As terrible as it may sound, it was a very practical way of disposing infected blood. Leeches are used even today but mostly for the purpose of reconstruction. They are used to suck blood through veins and arteries that have just been reattached.

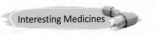

93 Is it possible to look exactly like someone else these days ?

Cosmetic surgery has come a long way. Not only is it possible to tweak your looks, it is also possible to make yourself look like someone else. And today, it is even possible to do a full face transplant. Does that mean you can look like your favourite movie star? Well, not really. Not unless they are willing to donate their face to you. A full face transplant would imply that the face and facial muscles are donated by the donor, to be surgically attached to your face so that you can look like the donor. Even then, the wounds have to heal and your body has to accept the new tissue. After that, there is a possibility that you might look like your donor. However, your donor might not look like the donor anymore!

94 — How are maggots useful medically ?

One of the grossest moments of your childhood would be to bite into an apple and find a maggot in it. If it hasn't happened to you, it has happened to someone you know. However, these creatures are quite useful and come in very handy medically speaking. Maggots are the larvae of your regular housefly that thrive on rotting meat. Surgeons use them to clean a wound that has been infected. The maggots eat away at the infected flesh leaving the wound clean and ready to heal using medication or surgery.

95 — Why is it important for a baby to be fed on mother's milk for the first 6 months ?

A newborn baby is very delicate. As soon as it is born, it needs to build resistance to all the microorganisms that are present outside the mother's womb. The best and only way to do this is through mother's milk. It is said that mother's milk has a substance called 'Hamlet' i.e., human alpha-lactalbumin made lethal to tumour cells. This not only protects the child against cancer in the future, but researchers at the Lund University and the University of Gothenburg of Sweden have found that it could possibly even cure cancer. This substance can destroy cancer cells! This is why a baby must always be fed on its mother's milk till it turns 6 months old.

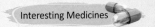

96 Is there a surgery that can increase one's height?

People come in all shapes and sizes, and of varied height. Your shape and size can be tweaked either naturally or through plastic surgery. However, you couldn't do much about height. If you wanted to be an airhostess, or wanted to serve in the military, you naturally had to be of a certain height, or tough luck. But today, cosmetic surgery has evolved so much that a person's height can be altered too. This is done by fracturing the outer layer of the bones of the thigh and using metal braces to stretch the bone. The outer layer then heals around the stretched bone. The process is then repeated. In this way, the height of your body can be increased.

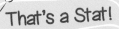
That's a Stat!

Bone lengthening is recommended up to 5 cm by fracturing the bone of the thigh. However, people have become up to 12 cm taller by fracturing the bone of their shin as well!

97 Why do some cosmetics advertise having pearls in their products?

Pearls are beautiful little beads that women wear in the form of jewellery. They are organic substances that are created when a grain of sand gets trapped in an oyster. The organism covers it in a fluid called nacre to prevent the grain of sand from pricking it. But according to Chinese tradition, pearls are also used in powder form. Apparently, they are very good for your skin and one can not only avoid acne and other skin issues, but it also increases the life of the skin cells. This powder is also known to have properties that can keep your skin from aging. No wonder that they are such a hit in the cosmetic industry.

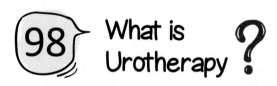

98 What is Urotherapy?

Urotherapy is the use of urine as medicine. This may seem like a disgusting idea, however, it is said that urine contains antibodies that are very beneficial to the human body. Antibodies are elements in the body that fight disease and protect it from cancer, AIDS, etc. They build your resistance and immunity. Although this is the belief amongst users of this therapy, there has been no scientific research undertaken on the subject. This is also one of the reasons that medical authorities and institutions don't comment on it and maintain a neutral position towards urotherapy.

(99) Why do some hospitals have cryogenic chambers ?

The term cryogenic brings to mind stories of superheroes who were frozen only to be thawed out years later. What would such a sci-fi object have to do in a hospital in today's day and age? As it happens, cryogenic chambers are very useful in deadening pain. When your body hurts, you rub ice on the sore muscles, numbing the pain and causing it to lessen or stop. Cryogenic chambers use liquid nitrogen to bring the temperature of the body under freezing point. Even athletes use this chamber to speed up the healing process of their bodies.

100 Why do ancient surgeries show doctors making a hole in people's skull

Surgery is a highly complex procedure that can be carried out by only a few people in the world. However, it is also one of the oldest medical procedures in the world. Doctors have been carrying out surgeries on their patients for over 7000 years. Whether all those patients survived or not is a story for another time. A popular practice at that time was to make a tiny hole in the skull of the patient. This is called Trepanation. Some doctors followed this procedure for medical and scientific reasons to relieve cranial pressure or to inspect the brain. Others used it to release evil spirits they believed to be trapped in the patient's brain.

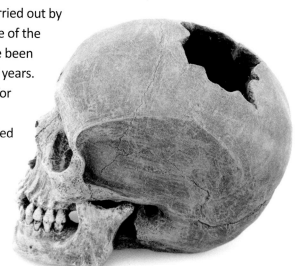

101 How did poisonous mercury come to be a part of medicine history

Today, we know that mercury is poisonous and should not be ingested. However, in olden times, it was used to treat minor infections. People ingested mercury as medicine, that is until it started having an effect on their kidneys, causing them to fail. Since then, mercury is used very sparingly and avoided in medicines.

The Chinese were so impressed with mercury that they used it to create the elixir of life, a liquid meant to make the drinker immortal! Unfortunately, the Chinese Emperor Qin Shi Huang tried this elixir and passed away. They probably gave up the idea of magical elixirs after that.

102 When were diet pills invented ?

Believe it or not, diet pills have existed since the 1920s. Although there is insufficient proof of this, there are advertisements for diet pills dating back to the early 20th century. Most of them caused side effects like headaches and fevers, while others were highly addictive. But the worst of them all were the ones that contained dehydrated tapeworms or tapeworm eggs. Tapeworms are parasites that grow within your intestine, feasting on the food and nutrition that you eat. This causes malnutrition in your body leading to weight loss. Tapeworms can grow up to several feet long inside your body.

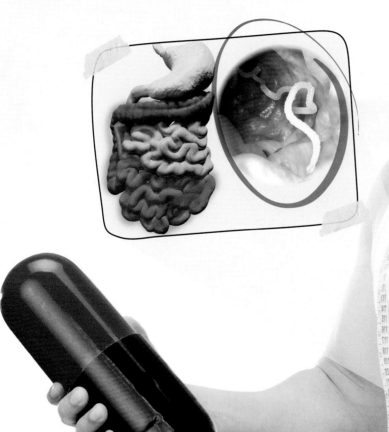

103 What is the most repulsive thing that can be in your face pack

With more and more people becoming conscious about their looks, skincare has become a booming industry. There are so many products in the market, yet there is a constant search for newer and better ingredients that can be added to face products; papaya, aloe vera, nut butters, and various other organic materials. However, a spa in New York has taken it to another level. They provide a special facial called the Geisha Facial that includes a nightingale's droppings as a special component!

104 What is the weirdest ointment to be used on wounds

Historically speaking, there have been many practices that would be considered a hazard nowadays. One of the major issues that doctors faced in olden times was disinfecting a wound. Basic disinfection was a matter struggled with and so many different techniques were used. We have already read about the use of mouldy bread for this purpose. The other weird things consisted of mice meat, reptilian blood and even the saliva of various animals. These were used because of the bacteria in them that fought harmful microorganisms. But at the end of the day it was always a matter of the good bacteria outweighing the bad bacteria in the application. However, the winner of the weirdest ointment award goes to animal dung used for its antibiotic properties.

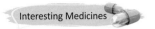

105 Have live animals ever been a part of treatment ?

Till a few years ago, skincare was either organic or chemical. While no live animals were used, parts of their bodies may have been. However, in recent years, live fish have been introduced for facial skin treatment and pedicures as well. The Garra rufa fish are small carps that eat dry skin or damaged skin in case of skin diseases, on the face and feet. The face or the feet are dipped in a tub with a school of Garra rufa and they exfoliate your skin like nothing else can. No wonder they are also known as 'Doctor Fish'.

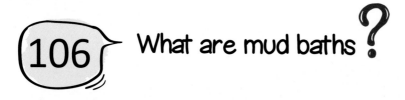

106 What are mud baths?

There are natural ponds full of mud all around the world. This mud is made up of a special kind of clay with healing properties and minerals that bring a shine to your skin. The clay is packed with nutrients that improve the health of the skin by exfoliating, soothing as well as disinfecting the epidermis. Some clays are good to reduce the body heat and cool down the skin. In tropical countries, these clays are very relaxing. How would you like to swim in a mud pond for better skin?

107 Can bee stings cure cancer ?

A bee's sting contains venom that causes pain and swelling when it punctures your skin. However, there are people who believe that this venom is actually helpful and can cure various medical conditions. Haj Mohamed el-Minyawi is one such person who believes that bee venom consists of a special protein which is capable of curing diseases like asthma, rheumatism and even cancer. Scientifically, there is no research or survey to prove that this is useful, but many people undergo this treatment in the belief that the bee sting can cure their ailments.

108 How does the cupping therapy work ?

We live in such a fast world that a lot of people are constantly stressed out and end up carrying this stress around in the muscles of their back or neck. There are many therapies available today to help with stress-release. One such therapy is cupping. The procedure consists of heating little glass cups with small mouths till all the air inside them has been pushed out. They are then applied to the painful area of the body causing the vacuum to pull at the muscles. This works on the deeper muscles in the body, causing heat and pressure to reach the muscles of the back and neck that are stressed and soothe them.

109 What is the 'Medicine Festival' of India ?

The Medicine Festival happens every June in Hyderabad.
A family in a small city in Hyderabad claims to be able to
cure people of asthma and other ailments by pushing
live fish down their throats! The miracle fish medicine is
administered free of cost. It is given on specific days. The
fish is first stuffed with a yellow herbal paste, the contents
of which are a family secret. Apparently, the formula of the
herbal paste was given to the family by a saint in 1845. The
saint was so impressed with the generous nature of one of
the ancestors, that he parted with the secret formula for
this amazing cure. It has been handed down from father
to sons over the ages. Not your roll of sushi, is it?

110 What is DNA therapy ?

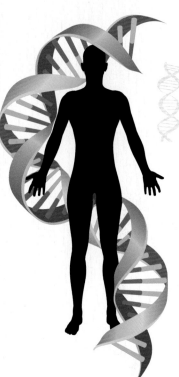

There is a theory in medical science that some emotional behaviours are hereditary and are passed down from generation to generation because of the information stored in DNA. DNA therapy involves recognising these traits and taking counter measures towards repetitive behaviours. This includes positive reinforcements for behaviour that you would want continued and negative ones for the chain of behaviour that you would like to break. Addictive, violent and insecure traits are some of the many that can be changed due to DNA therapy. This therapy does not make any changes to your basic DNA.

111 How does sticking needles in your body help your health ?

The process of using tiny needles to puncture the skin in order to stimulate certain nerve endings is called acupuncture. It works on the basis of the concept of the energy of life. According to the Chinese, energy constantly flows through our body affecting our thoughts and moods. Acupuncture can create a change in this flow of energy, causing any negative energy or diseases to be corrected, and hence cure the body of any health issues. People suffering from great stress and depression, seek this therapy as it helps the body as well as the mind to relax. Do you feel like some needles in your back, today?

112 Is beer good for your skin?

Using beer to wash your hair has become a thing of the past. Its effervescence makes your hair feel soft and conditioned. These days, beer has been taken a step further. If it can affect the keratin of your hair, imagine how well it will affect the live cells of your skin! Today, you will find beer spas in the Czech Republic, where customers can relax and feel calm in a tub of beer. It is soothing and exfoliates the skin, because of its effervescent property. It also helps you to de-stress as the alcohol in it gets sponged up by your skin.

113 What is Rebirthing therapy?

The Rebirthing therapy is simply a reenactment of the time when you were born with the help of breathing exercises. According to administrators of the rebirth therapy, we are in a warm tight and comfortable place when we are conceived, lulled into safety by constantly listening to the heartbeat of our mother. When we are pushed out into the world, it is a huge shock. We get used to this, but when life becomes too stressful, its effects can be reversed by going back to the comfort of being in your mother's womb. That is also why we rock ourselves when we are grieving. It is because the body goes back to following the rhythm of the heartbeat that it is used to in the mother's womb. This is also why we curl up in a foetal position when we are in pain.

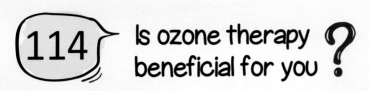

114 Is ozone therapy beneficial for you?

This therapy is highly controversial. Because according to medical authorities, ozone is toxic. Oxygen is a life giver. But an additional atom of O per molecule of O2 makes ozone. The ozone layer around the Earth may protect us from the harmful UV rays of the Sun, but when brought in contact with the human body, is harmful. However, propagators of ozone therapy seem to believe that ozone therapy can not only cure cancer, but also AIDS and other major medical conditions. They use injections, saunas and other ways to introduce ozone gas into the body. The user feedback is at the moment undecided.

115 How do scents help in healing ?

The process of using scents and aromas to help and encourage healing in a patient is called aromatherapy. Aromatherapy is a researched and studied procedure in which various scents and fragrances are used to soothe the mind as well as the body. This is often paired with acupressure where different points of the body are pressurised to release the stress from the muscles. A person's sense of smell has a direct connection to their emotions and aromatherapy works on this basis. Many mental issues like anxiety, depression and grief can be treated using aromatherapy.

116 Is a brain transplant possible ?

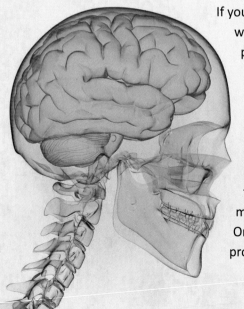

If you have a computer and it stops working, what do you do? IT help can probably pull out the motherboard and fit it into another computer with a brand new body. So why can't we do the same? Imagine if we could take out one person's brain and fit it into another body! Although theoretically possible, practically, it is another story. Putting together severed nerves is something that medicine is struggling with at the moment. Once we have a breakthrough, you could probably buy a new body online!

117 Why is Ayurvedic medicine so popular these days ?

Ayurvedic medicine, is medicine that is made on the basis of medical scriptures written by Indian saints many years ago. These scriptures were called Ayurveda and hence the medicine came to be known as Ayurvedic medicine. Along with being completely organic, this alternative treatment focussed on treating the mind and the soul along with the body. In today's world where people are worried about their mental health along with their physical health this medication comes as a life saver.

There isn't much in the form of evidence that this treatment works, but considering the fact that it is so old, and has been carried out for such a long time, there could be something to it.

118 How did dentists treat people in the olden days ?

Back in the olden days, when medicine was not as advanced as it is today, people often ended up treating the symptoms of the problem rather than the problem itself. Toothache was treated with numbing elements such as eucalyptus oil and rubbing salt on the teeth. If the tooth got worse, it was knocked out! This happened often since dental hygiene was not a priority as it is today. People brushed their teeth with burnt herbs. Alcohol was used as mouthwash. Forget about a pearly white smile you'd be lucky to have all your teeth by the time you grew up.

119 Why can't we lower our blood pressure if it is too high ?

Blood pressure is controlled by our heartbeat and the heart beats on its own, involuntarily. That is the reason why we cannot control our blood pressure. However, there is a process by which we can take control of all the involuntary processes of the body like breathing, heart rate, blinking, etc., known as biofeedback. Biofeedback therapists train their patients to keep calm, relax their breathing and perform mental exercises. Beginners are hooked onto monitoring devices, but as they improve, they can practice this therapy on their own. Research states that this treatment works as many of the ailments are caused are due to stress.

120 Does water have healing properties ?

There are many places around the world that claim that the water of a certain river or stream has magical healing properties. But, normal water by itself is beneficial for the body. It helps in flushing out waste from the body and regulates its temperature. Due to this, water is also used in therapy, known as water therapy or balneotherapy.

Balneotherapy takes it a step further claiming that it can strengthen immunity and hence it is administered in the form of wraps, baths and mudpacks. Like all alternative treatments, research on this therapy too is inconclusive. However, it shouldn't stop you from continuing with your daily intake of water.

121 Was body odour as big an issue in olden days as it is today

Deodorants as you all know were invented very recently and although perfumes have existed since ages, they were accessible only to the rich. That does not mean that body odour wasn't a problem back then. In fact, it was an even bigger problem than it is today, because bathing every day was not in fashion. People smelled pretty bad and to mask it, they carried nosegay flowers. And if you thought that the rich were sorted because of perfume, you'd be wrong. They smelled just as bad, because of the layers of clothes they wore under their day clothes. Thank god for deodorant and better hygiene!

122 Why did old asylums deprive their patients of sleep ?

Asylums were one of the worst places to be in prior to the advancement of medicine. The treatments that the doctors recommended were nothing less than torture and would often make one question the sanity of the doctors themselves! The Camarillo Mental Hospital of California experienced overcrowding in the olden days and had an insufficient number of beds for their patients. They came up with the idea of making their patients take turns using the bed and sleeping. Later, they found that the lethargic state that the patients went in to, on being sleep deprived, was good to keep them under control and apparently also helped their depression. As it turned out later, it in fact worsened the mental health of the patients.

123 Do surgeons really forget their instruments inside patients ?

It sounds like the beginning of a joke, but it happens more often than you would expect. There are about 1500 reports of surgical instruments getting left inside a patient during the surgery. Most of the time it is the surgical sponge. Whether this is due to sheer oversight and forgetfulness, or it does have a justifiable reason, is not known as yet. A case in point is of Nelson E. Bailey. His intestine was being operated upon when the surgeon forgot a foot-long sponge inside him. Imagine something as long as a subway sandwich stitched into your stomach cavity! Bailey had to be operated upon again and the sponge taken out.

124 Why is electricity used as a part of treatment ?

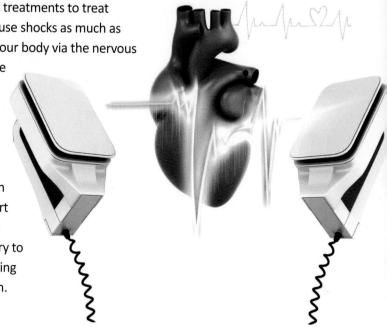

In the old days many asylums used shock treatments to treat their patients. However, today, we don't use shocks as much as tiny electric impulses. Our brain controls our body via the nervous system. Various organs work based on the little impulses that the brain sends to the rest of the body and organs to carry out everyday duties. Sometimes due to damage to the nerves, the impulse centre of the nerves stop working. Electric current of very low voltage is then passed through these centres to jumpstart them back to life just like you jumpstart a car battery. This is also how the doctors try to get a heart that has stopped to start beating again. It doesn't work all the time, though.

125 What were the soothing syrups administered to children in olden days ?

Seeing many children around you and most of them crying a lot, makes you wish you could give them something to calm them down. In the 19th century people had a soothing syrup for children that would help them relax and often go to sleep. Any child who was hyperactive or naughty was made to take this soothing syrup which made them feel drowsy. The main component of this syrup was opium. This not only made the child fall asleep, but was also highly addictive causing children to have withdrawal symptoms when they stopped the medication. Needless to say, people stopped using it (and doctors stopped administering it) when its negative effects were revealed.

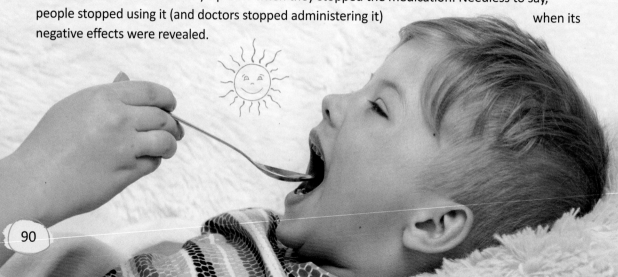

Spaced Out Facts

At some point in life, each one of us has gazed at the stars in a black night sky and felt so small compared to the vast universe that stretches around us. There is so much to be learnt about this infinite space around us. Some of these things are interesting, others are shocking. Let's take a look at our universe and get a bit spaced out!

126 How does zero-gravity affect the skin of astronauts ?

On the Earth, there are many factors that bring about changes to our skin. There is heat, and wear and tear that makes us sweat and maintain the moisture of our skin. However, in space, astronauts are in zero-gravity. They don't use their feet a lot. This causes the skin of their feet to dry and peel off. Since water is used very sparingly in space, astronauts tend to wear the same clothes and socks for long spells of time. When they finally take off their socks to wear new ones, their feet have shed a considerable amount of skin cells. This is why they have to take them off carefully. If skin cells escape, they keep floating in zero-gravity and may block important vents causing technical issues.

127 What is the hottest planet of our Solar System?

One would assume that since the Sun is the source of all the heat in the Solar System, any planet closest to it would have to be the hottest as it would receive the most amount of heat from the Sun. But the problem with Mercury being the hottest planet is that it heats up and loses heat very quickly. This raises its temperature to 425°C every day and drops it to -180°C every night. However, Venus has an atmosphere and thick clouds that trap the heat giving it a heat margin of 500°C, making it the hottest planet of the Solar System.

128 How long is a day on Venus?

A day on a planet is determined by how long it takes to rotate. For example, the Earth takes 23 hours 56 minutes and 4 seconds to rotate on its axis. This determines the length of our day, which is 24 hours. Similarly, Venus spins on an axis too. The only difference being that it takes 243 Earth days to complete one revolution. However, it also takes 224.7 days to rotate on its axis. This means that a day on Venus is longer than a year on the Earth. It also means that a day on Venus is longer than a year on Venus itself! It takes longer for the planet to complete a full rotation than it takes for the planet to orbit around the Sun!

129 What is the weather like on other planets ?

The weather is always something to complain about. It's either too hot or too cold or too wet. But what we have here on the Earth is paradise as compared to the weather on other planets. Some of these include Jupiter that has raging hurricanes lasting over 300 years. It gets extremely hot and extremely cold on Mars and Mercury in the duration of the same day. And Venus is even hotter than that! There are continuous gales on the surface of Saturn, Uranus and Neptune. Neptune being one with the fastest gales.

130 How does space travel affect our body ?

As people who are used to gravity, it is very difficult to imagine the effect zero-gravity could have on our body. The difference between the two situations is similar to carrying a boulder on your shoulder at all times and walking empty-handed. The simplest effect to understand is that since gravity doesn't pull us downward all the time, we tend to be able to stand straight and tall. Our spine gets straightened out, resulting in us becoming a few cm taller. Now you know what to do when you want to look taller!

131 How far away is space?

When you imagine huge planets and uncountable celestial bodies that look like twinkling points in the sky, you feel that space is very far away from you.

However, in all practicality, space begins from what is known as the Karman Line. This imaginary line goes around the Earth and is 100 km away from its surface at all points. This basically means that if you could manage to build a ladder 100 km in length and climb to its highest rung, you would technically be in space! Would you like to give that a shot?

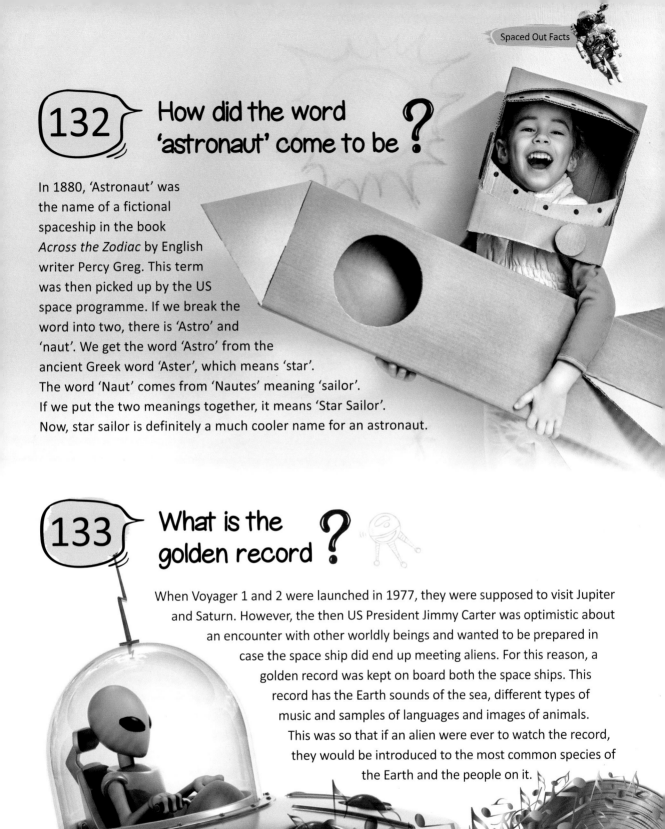

132 How did the word 'astronaut' come to be ?

In 1880, 'Astronaut' was the name of a fictional spaceship in the book *Across the Zodiac* by English writer Percy Greg. This term was then picked up by the US space programme. If we break the word into two, there is 'Astro' and 'naut'. We get the word 'Astro' from the ancient Greek word 'Aster', which means 'star'. The word 'Naut' comes from 'Nautes' meaning 'sailor'. If we put the two meanings together, it means 'Star Sailor'. Now, star sailor is definitely a much cooler name for an astronaut.

133 What is the golden record ?

When Voyager 1 and 2 were launched in 1977, they were supposed to visit Jupiter and Saturn. However, the then US President Jimmy Carter was optimistic about an encounter with other worldly beings and wanted to be prepared in case the space ship did end up meeting aliens. For this reason, a golden record was kept on board both the space ships. This record has the Earth sounds of the sea, different types of music and samples of languages and images of animals. This was so that if an alien were ever to watch the record, they would be introduced to the most common species of the Earth and the people on it.

134 What is cold welding?

Due to the lack of oxygen in space, any two metal items of the same element would fuse together and become inseparable. This is called cold welding. That is how metals behave naturally when there is a lack of oxygen. Imagine all the coins in your pocket sticking to each other, or the cutlery in your kitchen drawers fusing together. On the Earth, our metals don't fuse because of the presence of oxygen in our atmosphere. When astronauts leave the Earth's atmosphere an oxide layer is maintained around their tools to keep them from welding together.

135 What is a Supermoon?

That's a Stat!
We have been lucky to witness the Supermoon very recently. The moon came the closest to the Earth on 14th November, 2016. Next, it will be that close only on 25th November, 2034.

We know that the moon revolves around the Earth just like the Earth revolves around the Sun. Also, in both the cases, the paths of their orbits are elliptical. Due to this shape of the orbit, the moon comes closer to the Earth. This is when the moon appears bigger to us. When this event coincides with a full moon, we have a Super-moon that looks about 14 per cent bigger. Unrelated to this, there is also an optical illusion that the moon looks bigger at the horizon. The moon isn't actually bigger, it simply appears so, as we tend it to the buildings and trees that we see on the horizon. So the moon not only has different shapes but also comes in various sizes!

136 Why do the Saturn rings disappear periodically ?

In 2009, when Saturn was observed through a small telescope, one couldn't see its rings. However, it was discovered that this is an ongoing illusion that seems to occur every 14-15 years. This happens because, every time Saturn goes around the Sun, it aligns itself in such a way that it faces the Earth edge-on. Only the edge of the rings is visible, if at all, to an observer on Earth. It is the same principle as looking at a leaf of paper with its edge towards you. A two-dimensional object seems to disappear. That is how Saturn seems to take off its rings every 14-15 years.

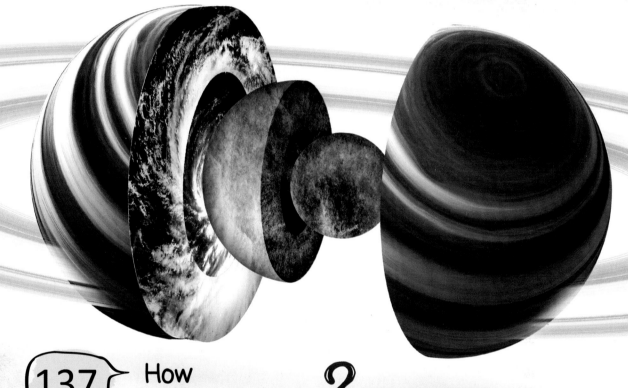

137 How dense is Saturn ?

Saturn is a very low-density planet. Although the core of the planet consists of heavy metals, the outer surface of the planet is made up of hydrogen gas making it one of the least dense planets to be known. The density of Saturn is 0.687 g/cm^3. This is even lower than the density of water which is 0.998 g/cm^3. Due to this property, if we were to magically produce a glass full of water big enough to hold the planet Saturn, technically, the planet would float!

138 How is the first footprint left by an American astronaut still on the moon?

One of the reasons why the moon-landing has been said to be a hoax by conspiracy theorists is because of the footprint on the moon. How was it formed if the moon has no gravity? How is it still there? The fact is that the moon does have gravity, only it is much weaker than Earth's. So it is quite possible the footprint was formed on the surface of the moon. Now, if you are wondering how the footprint managed to stay in place for so long, the answer is the weakness of the moon's gravity. This is also the reason why the moon has no atmosphere. No winds blow the dust from the surface of the moon and hence the footprint has remained intact.

 **Why do Mercury and Venus not have moons ?**

We know that almost all the planets in our Solar System have moons. Then why would Mercury and Venus be the only two planets without any moons? The answer is simple. It is because they are the closest planets to the sun. Any moon that ever formed around Mercury or Venus would be pulled into the strong gravity of the Sun or else, if they were orbiting too close to the planets then they would get destroyed due to the tidal gravitational forces. You can't help feeling sad for these lonely planets, can you?

 **Is there a planet made out of diamonds ?**

55 Cancri e is a planet that is visible to the naked eye from Earth. It is composed almost entirely of carbon in the form of graphite and diamonds where Earth is composed of oxygen and water. This planet is twice the size of Earth, and its surface is peppered with the precious substance that is so well known on Earth as diamonds. This planet orbits the Sun at a very high speed putting a year on the planet to 18 hours only! Scientists believe that this hyper-speed planet will not last long.

141 Is there water in Space ?

Space is a vacuum and so it doesn't hold water on its own. However, astronomers keep finding new things and they have found a huge cloud in space which is made up of water vapour. It is estimated that this cloud holds enough water to fill the Earth's ocean 140 trillion times! This cloud surrounds a quasar, a huge active black hole. The cloud is more than 12 billion lightyears away from the Earth. It is believed that the components formed and manipulated around the black hole is creating this water resulting in the huge water vapour cloud.

142 How fast are we moving in Space ?

Stand still, very still. Now think. We are on a planet that is rotating on its own. It is also revolving around the Sun. Not just that, the whole Solar System is hurtling forward in space, planets and all! Now consider the fact that the Milky Way Galaxy, to which our Solar System belongs is also spinning on its own at 225 km per second! Do you really think you are standing in the same place? On Earth, yes but in space, you are at least 19 thousand km away from where you were a minute ago!

143 Is Uranus known by any other name?

Uranus was the first planet that was discovered using a telescope. It was discovered in 1781, by Sir William Herschel, who was also given the honour of naming the planet as he chose. At that time, the fashion was to name the planets after Greek gods like Mars, Mercury, Venus, Jupiter, Saturn and so on. Sir Herschel, however, wanted to name it after something that would help one remember when it was discovered. He therefore called it George's Star after his supporter King George III. In this way one would remember that the planet was discovered during the reign of King George III. And that is why Uranus was originally called George's star.

144 How much space debris is present around the Earth ?

With the success of Sputnik, all the countries entered the space race trying to launch a successful excursion into space. Many succeeded. However, many of the old and non-functional spaceships and satellites launched from the Earth's atmosphere end up in a huge cloud of space debris around the Earth, just above its atmosphere. This includes discontinued satellites, the launch packs of space vehicles, broken bits from the wear and tear of vehicles as they entered and left Earth's atmosphere, specks of paint and even little ice-clouds. About half a million pieces of space debris is estimated to be floating around the Earth.

145 How does Space Debris affect Space Travel ?

Of all the debris present in the lower-orbit of the Earth, there are about 1 million pieces of debris that are smaller than 1 cm. These travel around the Earth at the rate of approximately 7 km per second. That is almost like half a Grand Piano coming towards you at 60 km per hour! At this speed, even a tiny fleck of paint can put a dent if not breach the outer shell of a Space Vehicle, the results of which could be catastrophic. Space agencies on Earth maintain a vigilance through a radar and track all these pieces of space debris, including the million 1 cm pieces. When a spacecraft is launched, it is manoeuvred in such a way that it doesn't hit any of the debris.

146 Is the moon drifting away from the Earth ?

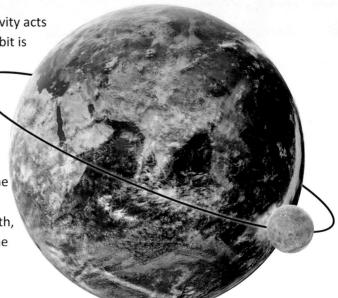

As the moon revolves around the Earth, its gravity acts on Earth and vice versa. However, since this orbit is elliptical, the force of gravity projected by each object on the other varies. It is due to this constant increase and decrease in the gravitational pull that, the moon is slowly moving further away from the Earth. Every year, the moon's orbit around the Earth shifts outwards by 3.8 cm. It is believed that the orbit of the moon will keep shifting outwards till it is beyond the gravitational pull of the Earth, and the moon will either drift away or enter the gravitational pull of another planet.

147 Do the heavenly bodies have any effect on the music created on Earth ?

The heavenly bodies are at extremely large distances away from the Earth. The Sun, however, has a part to play in its musical history. It seems that from the 1500s to the 1800s, the Earth went through an ice age because the solar activity reduced. The trees that grew at this time grew very slowly and had hard trunks. Centuries later, Antonio Stradivari used these trees to make violins that turned out to be masterpieces, as hard wood works well for violins. And hence, the famous Stradivarius violins were produced.

148 How big is the Sun ?

The Sun is 695,700 km across. To give you a perspective of this, consider 1.3 million Earths and put them together to form a ball. That is how big the Sun is. If we take a look at our Solar System and how vast it is, then the Sun itself accounts for 99.8 per cent of the mass in the entire Solar System! This means that all the planets, moons, stars and other celestial bodies in the Solar System only account for 0.2 per cent of the total mass of the Solar System!

149 How old is the sunlight that reaches us ?

We already know that sunlight takes eight minutes to reach the Earth. But before sunlight leaves the Sun, it is created at the core of the Sun where the temperature reaches around 15 million degrees Kelvin (K)! Sunlight is the energy which is formed at this core and then travels outwards towards the surface of the Sun. At this point, it has to pass through so many dense layers of gases that it takes

30,000 years just to travel from the core to the surface of the Sun. So, should we say that the sunlight we get today is 30,000 years old?

150 Is the Sun diminishing

The Sun is losing mass due to two reasons; solar winds and fusion reactions. Solar winds push away all the charged particles that lie on the surface of the Sun, resulting in a loss of up to 1.5 million tonnes per second. Besides, fusion reactions occurring at the core of the Sun creates heat energy. This means that the Sun's mass gets converted into energy which causes the Sun to lose about 4 million tonnes of mass per second. Yes, eventually, the Sun will diminish, however, it will be trillion of years before that happens.

151 Do we live inside the Sun ?

We think of the Sun as a heavenly body that is millions of kilometres away from us. However, we technically live within the Sun's atmosphere. The outer atmosphere of the Sun extends way beyond its visible surface. It is the solar wind that blows from its surface that gives us the Northern and Southern lights. However, not only are these lights visible on Earth but also on Jupiter, Saturn, Uranus and the distant planet Neptune. It is believed that the Sun must have a tail, as it is moving forward through space. This tail is believed to extend to hundreds of billion kilometres, which is enough not only to engulf our planet but also to cover the entire Solar System!

152 Can we see millions of stars in the sky

You must have heard songs, poems or movies and commercials speaking about 'a million shiny stars in the sky'. The truth is that at any point of time, no matter how dark the sky is or which point of the mountain you are sitting on, there are, at best, 2000-2500 stars visible to the naked eye and that too, if the observer has very good eyesight. It would still be difficult for an observer to count all of them. So, the next time you see a starry sky and feel overwhelmed to talk or write about it, say thousands of stars instead of a million. Let's keep it real, shouldn't we?

153 Why do some stars twinkle and others don't ?

Stars, actually, don't twinkle at all! They simply appear to do so for a very simple reason. The star Sirius for example, twinkles so much that people often mistake it for an airplane or an UFO. The twinkling has nothing to do with the star itself. It simply emits light. But when this light passes through all the layers of the Earth's atmosphere, it bends and bounces off. This causes the light to appear 'broken' or twinkling as we call the stars. This bending and bouncing of the light often gives it a colour as well. Now that's a whole new take on your favourite nursery rhyme!

Are red stars the hottest and blue stars the coolest?

Since childhood we have associated red with hot and blue with cold. After all, it is 'red hot' and 'cool blue' isn't it? Actually, not when it comes to stars. It seems that when a star is hot, it glows red. As the temperature starts increasing, the colour changes to orange, yellow, white, and on further heating, it turns blue. They actually also turn green before they turn blue, but that is not visible to us, and our eyes perceive it as white. So the red stars you see are actually the least hot stars. The hottest stars are the blue ones!

Is the Sun the biggest star in the known universe?

No. And not even close! It is easy to assume that our Sun is the biggest star ever, as it dominates our sky during the day. However, of all the stars that we see at night, there are only a few as big as the Sun, the rest are even bigger! These stars are much farther away from us than the Sun, and hence they appear as mere pin pricks in the sky as opposed to the Sun that looks like a giant ball of fire. There are about 50 stars that are visible to the naked eye from the Earth. The least bright of them is Alpha Centauri, and even that star is 1.5 times as as the Sun. That should give you some perspective.

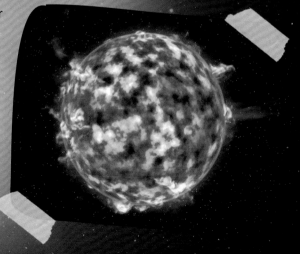

156 Do other planets have volcanoes?

This is a typical case in point where a familiar Earthly concept appears on another heavenly body and still is different in a basic way. We have volcanoes that erupt and spew magma. You must have seen videos of the red, hot, viscous liquid oozing out from cracks in a mountain. The same phenomena is present on Saturn's moon Enceladus, Neptune's moon Triton and so on. However, there is one minor difference. These volcanoes don't spew magma, they spew water! There are ice deposits under their mountains that get heated and blow out from the surface. We have smaller versions of these on Earth. We call them natural geysers.

That's a Stat!

Mars has a volcanic mountain called Olympus Mons. This mountain is 26 km high, towering at three times the height of Mt Everest!

157 How small is Pluto?

A few years ago, one of our beloved planets had to exit the list because of its size. Pluto has been officially taken off the list of planets in our Solar System because it is too small. But how small is too small? To give you a perspective, Pluto is smaller than Earth's natural satellite, the moon. At 1400 miles across, the moon is a far cry from Pluto. It is less than half the width of the United States of America! No wonder it had to step down as a planet. Pluto is now classified as a Dwarf Planet.

158 Do all heavenly bodies with moons qualify to be planets?

Often the ability of a planet to hold moons in its gravity and control their orbit was included in the definition of a true planet. It seemed reasonable since smaller planets like Venus and Mercury did not have moons, and the moons of Mars were tiny. However, it has been discovered that even small bodies are capable of having moons. In 1993, a 32 km wide asteroid was discovered and it had a 1.5 km wide moon. The asteroid's name was Ida, and it was discovered by the Galileo probe. Since then, the ability to hold moons has not been regarded as exclusive to planets.

159 How far is the end of the Solar System ?

One would consider the end of the Solar System to be just beyond Pluto, however, it extends further beyond that. The distance between Pluto and the edge of the Solar System is 1000 times the distance between the Earth and Pluto. Our Solar System includes more than the Sun and the eight planets. It includes the Kuiper Belt and the Kuiper Belt Objects that are released from it. It also includes Trans-Neptunian Objects as well as the vast Oort cloud. It is the Oort cloud that extends way beyond Pluto and pushes the edge of the Solar System so far away.

160 Which planet has the biggest ocean in our Solar System ?

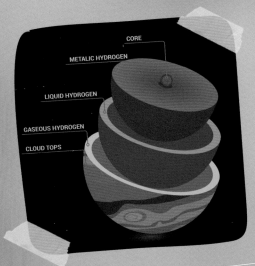

CORE
METALIC HYDROGEN
LIQUID HYDROGEN
GASEOUS HYDROGEN
CLOUD TOPS

There is a planet whose distance from the Sun is five times that of Earth. Hence in a relatively cooler climate as compared to Earth, this planet never lost its cloud of hydrogen and helium. In fact, this planet is made up mostly of these two elements. And because of the cold, the hydrogen in its atmosphere has been converted into liquid. So, this planet has an ocean of liquid hydrogen on its surface. This planet is none other than Jupiter. The ocean is deeper that 40,000 km, which is the width of our entire planet!

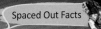

161 Do astronauts have to dodge asteroids when they are in space?

In many movies related to space travel, we see the spaceship enter an asteroid field and get bludgeoned by the burning rocks zooming through space. However, in the real world (or Space) the only existing asteroid belt that has been discovered so far is between Mars and Jupiter. There are a few thousand asteroids in this belt, however, they are so sparsely spaced that it is very improbable that a space ship would get hit by it. Our astronauts actually go seeking these asteroids so that they can photograph one!

162 Does Earth have alien material on it

From time to time, meteors in space get pulled in by the Earths' gravity, and land on the surface of our planet. These meteors could belong to any celestial body in space. There are some meteorite rocks that have been found in the Antarctica, the Sahara Desert and so on, that contain gases that resemble the chemical combination of the air present on Mars! This could be possible, as the meteorite could be a chunk of Mars that has broken away from it due to volcanoes, or another meteoroid or asteroid collision. These could then have entered the Earth's gravitational field and landed on the Earth.

163 In a hypothetical universal market how precious would Earth elements be

Our planet is full of elements like iron, oxygen, silicon, magnesium, sulphur, nickel, calcium, sodium and aluminium. They can also be found on other planets, however, only in traces. Other planets are heavily loaded with hydrogen and helium. There used to be an abundance of hydrogen and helium on the Earth as well. However, the Earth receives its heat from the Sun, and this heat heated up the light gases. Once hydrogen and helium were heated up, they became lighter and rose upwards into space. The hydrogen and helium cloud lifted off and floated away from our planet, leaving it full of rare metals.

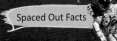

164 What is an asterism ?

Just like constellations, asterisms too are patterns formed in the sky by stars. However, asterisms are any other patterns that are not included in the list of 88 official constellations. Also, the stars of an asterism are far away from each other and are not related to each other physically. You might have traced out the Big Dipper on a starry night. However, the Big Dipper too is an asterism and not a constellation. Pegasus, the Great Diamond and the Winter Hexagon are some examples of asterisms.

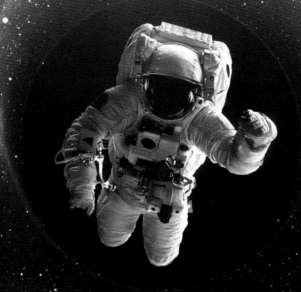

165 Do black holes suck in objects around them ?

Averse to popular notion that black holes are the naturally-occuring vacuum cleaners of the universe, the truth is that black holes don't actually suck in objects. There is no vacuum formed inside the black hole that allows any such reaction to be created. So what happens to things that get pulled into a black hole? These objects don't get 'sucked in' as much as they 'fall into' a black hole. Black holes are concentrated points of gravity so if a rock were to go into a black hole, it would be like, it were falling into a black hole not getting sucked into it.

Quirky Animals

We share this lovely planet with thousands of other species of living beings. They may not be as civilised as us, but some are quite intelligent. And there are those that are quirky, cute and simply outstanding. Let us introduce you to some of these gems that we share the Earth with.

166 How big can salamanders grow?

Salamanders are reptiles not unlike your ordinary home lizard, only bigger, more colourful and slimier. Now as much as we find their ordinary size intimidating, there are salamanders in China that grow as tall as an adult human being. Picture a six-foot long salamander sun-bathing in your garden! These Chinese salamanders, have extra skin on their body, through which they ooze a liquid that smells like pepper, to ward off predators. The extra skin also comes in handy as it helps absorb oxygen. Now why would a salamander need to absorb oxygen through its skin? To breathe, of course! Yes, salamanders are amphibians and breathe through their skin.

167 How strong is a spider web?

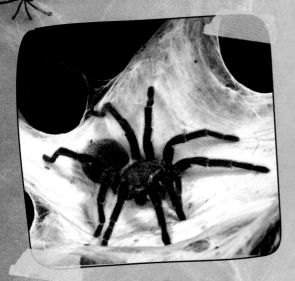

Different spiders weave different types of webs. Some spider webs are stretchy, others are strong, while a third variety makes up in size for what it cannot make up in strength. The Madagascar spider, is known to weave a web that is stronger than any other organic material in the world. Some say it is even stronger than Kevlar, which is used to make bulletproof fabric! Can you imagine a bulletproof vest made out of spider webs? Sometimes, these spiders weave a web that is big enough to cover two school buses. A perfect case of a strong, wonderful material being created by nature!

168 Are spiders stronger than snakes?

Snakes don't usually eat spiders when they require food. Similarly, spiders are known to trap flying insects in their web. However, there are spiders in Australia that attack and eat snakes. You would imagine a spider attacking a tiny water snake. But that is not always the case. Normal-sized snakes are attacked by these spiders, so you can imagine their size. These are hunter spiders, and don't always rely on their webs for trapping prey. They pounce and attack an unsuspecting snake. Often the snakes are ingested even when they are alive! It is quite terrifying down under, isn't it?

That's a Stat!

On an average the number of spiders found in green, grassy areas are about 50,000 per acre! If there is 3.5 billion acres of grassy land on the Earth, then you can calculate the number of spiders on this planet!

169 What is a salp ?

We often come across articles on the Internet about the excitement experienced by fishing folk on sighting a transparent fish in the ocean. Although it looks like an alien species with its internal organs on display, the fish is actually quite common in the ocean around the Antarctica. It is called salp. These fish swim along the surface of the ocean feeding on small marine animals and plants. Like any ordinary fish, salps also prefer swimming in groups. However, these fish form amazing, spiraling shapes in the water. What is even more amazing is that they function like trees underwater. By absorbing carbon dioxide and giving out oxygen, these fish maintain the levels of carbon dioxide underwater.

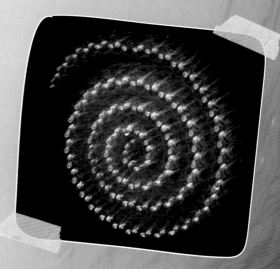

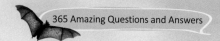

170 Can any animal survive freezing conditions ?

Isn't it common knowledge that if you are frozen solid, survival is difficult? Your blood freezes, all your body functions are arrested, and that is it. But the survival strategies of a little frog are unbelievable. Introducing the wood frog. This amazing frog, stores urea, a waste usually got rid of through the urine, in the cells of the body. The cells therefore don't freeze and are able to continue their functions. It also converts glycogen in its body to glucose for the same reason. This allows the frog to survive the cold months of winter, and thaw out during the spring, and go its own way!

171 Do self-healing animals exist ?

Healing yourself automatically would be quite a useful superpower to have in life, wouldn't it? You may have heard of reptiles that grow back entire body parts when they lose a tail or a limb. But have you heard of a frog that breaks its own toes to use the exposed bone as a weapon when in danger? This frog is known as the 'Horror frog'. Once the danger has passed, it heals itself again. Think of this creature as the Wolverine of frogs. Nature, aren't you scary?

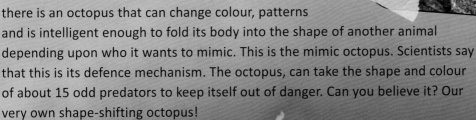

172 What is a mimic octopus?

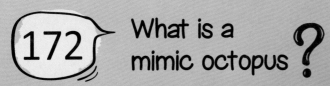

You've seen the regular octopus with its eight arms lined with tiny natural suction caps. Their movement is basically like a ball of slime rolling across the floor. However, there is an octopus that can change colour, patterns and is intelligent enough to fold its body into the shape of another animal depending upon who it wants to mimic. This is the mimic octopus. Scientists say that this is its defence mechanism. The octopus, can take the shape and colour of about 15 odd predators to keep itself out of danger. Can you believe it? Our very own shape-shifting octopus!

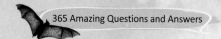

173 What is the loudest sound that an animal can make?

To give you a perspective of decibel levels, an aeroplane creates about 110 decibels of noise at takeoff. Now, we have a shrimp that can create up to 200 decibels of noise, which is almost the same as a dynamite explosion. But how can such a small creature create such a huge noise? What it does is, it attacks its prey with jets of water shooting from its claws. These jets are shot at 100 km/h and so they create air bubbles of low pressure. When these bubbles burst they create the explosive sound.

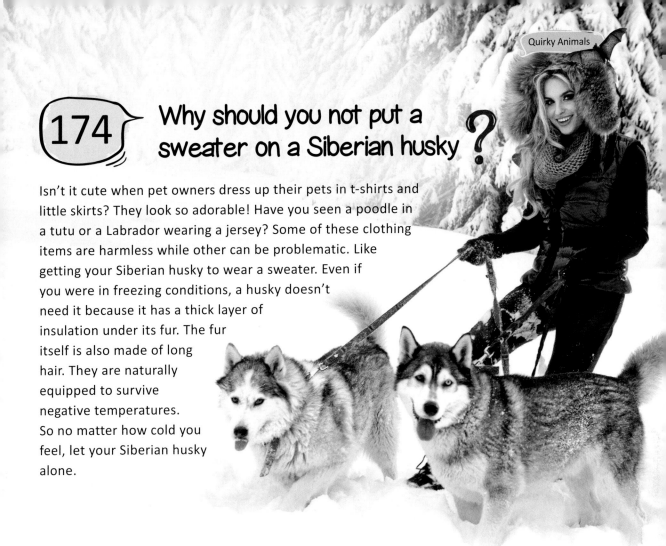

174 Why should you not put a sweater on a Siberian husky ?

Isn't it cute when pet owners dress up their pets in t-shirts and little skirts? They look so adorable! Have you seen a poodle in a tutu or a Labrador wearing a jersey? Some of these clothing items are harmless while other can be problematic. Like getting your Siberian husky to wear a sweater. Even if you were in freezing conditions, a husky doesn't need it because it has a thick layer of insulation under its fur. The fur itself is also made of long hair. They are naturally equipped to survive negative temperatures. So no matter how cold you feel, let your Siberian husky alone.

175 Are there animals that are immune to poison ?

So far we've heard of a self-healing frog, a shape-shifting octopus and a really loud shrimp. Comparatively, poison should be a piece of cake and we have a contender. The common opossums! They are annoying little things that like to go through garbage, and sneak into your home causing havoc, especially if you own a pet. However, these creatures are special in the sense that they are immune to poison. And not just the poison that it has had an encounter with, it has partial or total immunity to poisons that the opossum has never come in contact with before! Let's hope that whatever keeps these super creatures safe, can also be used to help people like you and me one day.

176 Are oysters male or female ?

Although it is very difficult to tell, oysters do have separate sexes and there are males as well as females of the species present. However, what makes it more confusing is that an oyster can change its gender more than once in its lifetime. All oysters are born males but within a year, their gender can change, and they may take up a different sex. This occurs based on the availability of male oysters and female oysters at the time of spawning. A male may turn into a female and even back to a male in its lifetime. Their genitalia becomes visible only during their mating season, and that is when you can tell if a certain oyster is male or female, although they may not stay that way forever.

177 Has there ever been a pig and sheep hybrid ?

Although scientists have been able to successfully create hybrids of many different species, there is no official record of a hybrid created from a sheep and pig. However, there is a breed of pig that basically looks like a pig with a thick layer of wool on its body, quite like that of a sheep! For quite some time people assumed them to be hybrids, but the truth is that they are simply a rare breed of pig. These are the Hungarian pigs called Mangalitsa, which are produced by cross-breeding Bakonyi and Szalontai breeds of pigs with Serbian Sumadia pigs. Pigs may not have been able to fly as yet, but at least they have got fluffy!

 **178** ## Were dinosaurs ever hunted by another species ❓

Yes. There was a species of reptiles that hunted dinosaurs. What could this species be that terrified even the dinosaurs? They were crocodiles! But, they were not your common crocodiles, they were galloping crocodiles! Paleontologists have found the fossils of crocodiles with longer legs that allowed them to gallop like a horse would. These fossils are more than a 100 million years old and dating around the same time as dinosaurs. Paleontologists found the fossils of these long-legged crocodiles in Morocco and Niger. Aren't you glad that they went extinct with the dinosaurs?

179 Why do Polar bears have white fur?

We all know that Polar bears are white. If there's a bear and it's white, then it's a Polar bear, right? You would actually be wrong to assume that. The fact is that Polar bears don't have white fur. Their hair is transparent! Polar bear hair lacks pigments and is actually hollow, which makes it transparent. So, all the white that we see is actually the snow reflecting off the hair. What's more is that the Polar bear skin under all the hair, is actually black!

180 What is the slowest fish in the sea ?

When we think of slow animals, tortoises, turtles, snails even slugs come to our mind. However, put these in water and they have a decent speed. Even turtles end up swimming faster in water. Most aquatic animals have streamlined bodies enabling them to move faster through the water. But the seahorse is one animal that moves in a different manner in water. Instead of cutting through the water, a seahorse moves upwards and downwards through the water at 0.01 mph.

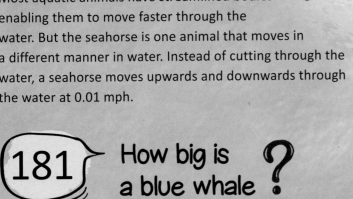

181 How big is a blue whale ?

That the blue whale is the biggest mammal in the world is a well known fact. But do you know how much it actually weighs? The average blue whale weighs a whopping 140,000 kg! That is equal to the weight of two Boeing 737 aircraft! Can you imagine a couple of aircraft merrily gliding under our oceans? Size-wise a blue whale is about 30 m long. That is roughly the size of an entire football ground. That said, the tongue of a blue whale itself is as heavy as one elephant. Can you imagine the weight of an elephant on your tongue?

182 How fast can ostriches run ?

Have you ever wished you could run as fast as the wind? Animals are fast when it comes to running, and they have to be fast, either to run away from predators or to catch their prey. One extremely fast runner is the ostrich. It runs at 70 km per hour when it is at its fastest. That is as fast as a car on a highway. When ostriches sense danger, they are known to bury their head in the sand thinking that no one can see them. Yet when it comes to flight, they run faster than horses. Besides when confronted, they are known to roar like lions to intimidate their pursuer. That's one bird I'd sure not like to mess with.

183 How do bats see ?

Bats are special in so many ways. Firstly, they are nocturnal animals. This means that while other animals sleep at night and wake up in the morning, these animals sleep in the morning and wake up at night. Secondly, they hang upside down from trees when resting. Thirdly, they are the only mammals that can fly. All living beings under the mammal category, are land or water animals. None of them are airborne, but bats are. Lastly, and most importantly, contrary to the popular belief, bats are not blind. They have well developed vision. They also have a keen sense of hearing. They emit sounds, and based on the feedback they get from the sound waves bouncing back, they navigate their way through air. It is a natural form of radar.

184 How long do houseflies live ?

An average housefly lives only up to 14 days. Within the span of a fortnight, the fly goes from a larva to a full grown adult. Can you imagine going from a wee baby to an elderly person in two weeks? Not just that, the houseflies also find time to reproduce in their short life span. But what about recreation? Flies have a talent for music. If you notice, they always hum in the key of F! Here's another fun fact. The mayfly has a lifespan of just one day!

185 How do puffins live?

As human beings, we consider ourselves so intelligent! We dominate the animal kingdom because we call ourselves civilised and take pride in the fact that we live in a 'society' bound by rules. But did you know, that a puffin's lifestyle is almost the same as us? They mate for life. They are loyal to a single partner. And when they have found them, they build a burrow in a cliff side, which becomes their home. Besides, they also mark out a separate place to be used as their toilets. If that isn't civilised, what is?

186 What determines a tiger's stripes ?

Take a close look at your fingertips and check out your fingerprints. You must already know that each fingerprint is unique. Similarly, tigers have their stripes. No two tigers will have the same stripes. Tiger stripes are almost as unique as our fingerprints. To top it off, the tiger's stripes are not based only on the colour of the fur. The skin under the fur is of the same colour as the fur. So, if we were to shave a tiger completely, we'd find that its skin too has stripes. This is because of different pigments present in different parts of the skin.

187 What is a crocodile's weak spot ?

Crocodiles, are one of the most lethal reptiles in the animal kingdom. Many people have lost their lives to these cold-blooded stalkers of the swamps. Their jaws are so strong that they clamp down on their prey like a bear trap would snap on an unsuspecting limb. Survival experts say that if someone were to find themselves trapped in the jaws of a crocodile, the best move would be to attack the crocodile's weak spots, which are its eyes. Putting pressure on the crocodile's eyes with your thumb ensures that its jaws go slack. This enables you to free yourself from its grip and make a hasty run for it.

188 How do kangaroos use their tails ?

Kangaroos are huge animals towering at over 6 feet while standing. They hop on two feet, but need help to balance. This is what they use their tail for. Their tail works like a tripod helping them stay erect, and maintaining their equilibrium while jumping and landing. So what would you do if you wanted to make a kangaroo stay in its place? You would lift its tail! A kangaroo never jumps if its tail isn't touching the ground. This could be because it uses the tail on the ground for the push off or simply to maintain balance.

189 Which animal can jump the highest ?

The red kangaroo is said to be able to jump over nine metres high. That is about the height of a two-storey building! However, if you take the size of the jumping animal in question, even the red kangaroo has competition from the tiny flea. A flea is a parasitic insect that feeds on the blood of its host. Anyone with a pet knows what a pain fleas can be. They jump from host to host, sucking blood. A flea is known to be able to jump to a height that is 200 times their own height. In human terms that would be like a man jumping to a height of about half a kilometre!

190 How can cats move their ears so much ?

If you own a cat, or even simply noticed one, you must have seen them move their ears. No matter which corner of the house they are in, the moment you put food in their plate, they hear you and come running for their daily meal. This is because a cat has 32 muscles in each ear. These muscles allow the ear to rotate and act like huge dish antennae that converge the sound waves. That is why a cat can bend and turn its ears around to catch sound of conversations, footsteps and the tinkling of its food dish whenever it wants to.

191 Why do Koala bears eat only eucalyptus leaves ?

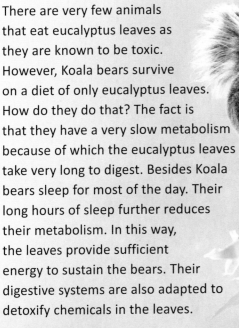

There are very few animals that eat eucalyptus leaves as they are known to be toxic. However, Koala bears survive on a diet of only eucalyptus leaves. How do they do that? The fact is that they have a very slow metabolism because of which the eucalyptus leaves take very long to digest. Besides Koala bears sleep for most of the day. Their long hours of sleep further reduces their metabolism. In this way, the leaves provide sufficient energy to sustain the bears. Their digestive systems are also adapted to detoxify chemicals in the leaves.

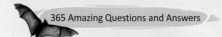

192 Are poodles French

Poodles are the daintiest dogs you will see. They are tall dogs with little round fluffs of fur around the body, limbs and tail. These elegant dogs were assumed to be from France. However, poodles are originally from Germany. This breed of dog was further developed in France to create its own version of poodles, which became quite popular. So yes, there are French poodles but they originated in Germany. Maybe you'd like to pick out a German name for your poodle rather than a French one.

193 Can butterflies see colours ?

Flowers are one of nature's most beautiful creations. They come in a variety of shapes and sizes and in many colours too. And fluttering gently over these flowers are the colourful butterflies. Wouldn't it be nice to have a pair of rainbow coloured wings, and fly amongst gardens full of scented flowers splashed with various colours? However, do you know that butterflies can see only three colours. Although they have compound eyes, butterflies can only see the colours red, green and yellow!

194 Why are ants said to be amazing creatures ?

If you have had the chance to observe an ant farm, you would observe that they are fascinating creatures. Not only can they work on their own, but they can hang onto each other and work as bigger objects in complete harmony. Other than that, they can pick up objects that are several times their own weight! They can even use the surface tension of the water to float by themselves or as a group like a raft. They perform many functions in nature like pollinating flowers, dispersing seeds and mixing nutrients in the soil.

195 How do giraffes deal with their long necks ?

Have you ever stood up suddenly after sitting down for a long time and felt light-headed? What happens is that when you get up quickly, your blood that has been at a certain height suddenly has to climb higher, and at a resting heart rate, your heart is unable to push it to your brain. The low blood flow to your brain makes you feel dizzy. Now, can you imagine what it must feel like for giraffes? It is a good thing that God gave them strong hearts that can pump blood all the way to the top of their heads to their brains.

196 What does a giraffe sound like ?

Elephants trumpet, monkeys chatter and horses neigh. But what does the giraffe say? Considering the long neck of a giraffe, you would think that it would sound quite exotic. But did you know that giraffes, in spite of the size of their necks, have no vocal chords at all? That is why they are mute. They cannot make any noise at all! They have a tongue that they use only for tasting, and unlike most other tongues that are a shade of pink or red, a giraffe's tongue is bluish-black in colour.

MUTE

197 — Why are dog's noses special

Dogs are truly man's best friends. Not only do they have instincts to recognise trouble, but they have the strongest and most powerful noses in the animal kingdom. You must have seen sniffer dogs that work with police to sniff out explosives, drugs and other materials with a scent or odour. But that is not the only reason why a dog's nose is special. If you've had the chance to take a look at a dog's nose at close range, you will see that it has tiny ridges, just like the tips of our fingers. And just like our fingerprints are unique, no two nose prints of a dog will ever be the same. Each dog has its own unique nose print that is actually used to identify them in vet records and pet adoption centres!

198 — How do squirrels help in forestation ?

With industrial development taking place at breakneck speed, forests are disappearing really fast. However, nature has a way of looking after itself. Different trees produce different seeds that find their way across the land. Animals and birds help in spreading these seeds faster and over distances. One such agent is the squirrel. Squirrels gather nuts and often bury them to hide. However, they often forget where they have buried these nuts. Unknowingly, the squirrels end up planting at least a million trees!

199 Why do beavers keep gnawing wood?

A beaver is a furry animal, the same size as an otter. We can recognise it by its two long front teeth. What comes to mind when you hear the word, 'beaver'? A dam! That is because beavers are famous for building dams. They pull together wood from the forest and shape it with their teeth to create a dam on rivers and streams. But why do they do that? A beaver has long teeth at the front. What's surprising about these teeth is that they never stop growing! So, it becomes necessary for beavers to keep chewing on things to keep their teeth from growing too long.

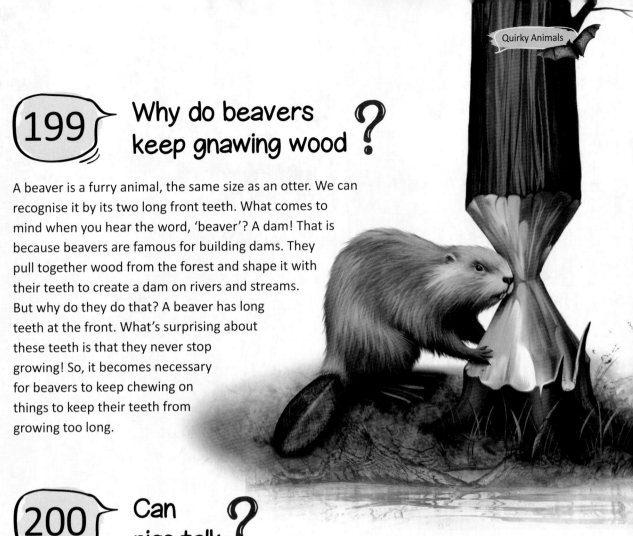

200 Can pigs talk?

All animals make some sort of noise or other. They use these noises to express emotions like anger, happiness, hunger, etc. However, pigs have an entire language. Pigs use grunts like humans use words. They have more than 20 grunt-words that they keep using in different circumstances. A few of their grunts have been recognised to mean various things like 'feed me' or something to call a mating partner. Pigs are constantly grunting and speaking to each other to co-ordinate or relay messages.

201 How fast does a hummingbird flap its wings ?

Hummingbirds are fascinating birds. They are the smallest among the bird species and they flap their wings so fast that it appears only as a blur to the naked human eye. On close observation, it has been determined that it beats its wings 80 times per second! Not only that, a humming-bird is the only bird that can fly backwards. The fast beating of its wings allows it to do that. This bird can also remain completely still in one spot in the air, while it sucks the nectar out of a flower.

 **Can animals have multiple hearts?**

The human body has one heart that pumps blood to every part of the body, from the top of your head to the fingers of your hands, to the toes of your feet. This heart takes in the de-oxygenated blood as well as pumps out the oxygenated blood. However, there are animals that have multiple hearts. Here, the functions of the heart are split up with a couple of hearts receiving the de-oxygenated blood and the other pumping out oxygenated blood. For example, the Cuttle fish has four hearts and the octopus has three.

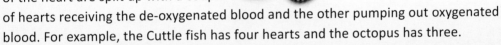

 **How do sea otters sleep?**

Otters are amongst the cutest animals on earth. These furry little critters have a shiny coat and are known for their playful nature, and their habit of somersaulting in water. There are land otters and sea otters. Sea otters have a waxy substance in their fur that doesn't allow water to stick to its body. They usually sleep on water. They just lie on their back and float on water. But how come they don't drift away? That is because they do something very cute. They hold the hands of other otters when they sleep so that all of them stay together and nobody drifts off into the sea!

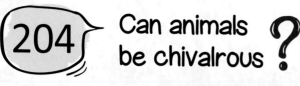

204 Can animals be chivalrous ?

Chivalry is dead, they say. But it doesn't matter if humans have forgotten this old code of conduct, the amazing thing is that animals follow it too. And what is more adorable than a pair of puppies playing and having fun with each other. It is often noticed that when a male puppy is playing with a female puppy, it will let the female puppy win even if the male puppy can win the game. Don't you wish average kids were that understanding?

205 How do caterpillars transform into butterflies ?

Everybody loves a good old makeover. That is the reason why we keep trying to change the way we look. However, the most notable transformation in the animal kingdom has to be of a caterpillar into a butterfly. So notable, in fact, that it is used as a metaphor in well-known literature. But what do you think happens inside the cocoon that the caterpillar spins around itself? Well, the body of the caterpillar dissolves. A pulp is formed from which a new shape emerges, that of a butterfly. Who said transformations are easy?

Terrific Trees & Plants

Trees add beauty to our planet Earth! We see them everywhere. They are vital for life on Earth, yet we often tend to take them for granted. Imagine a world without trees? There are some trees that are one-of-a-kind, too unique and unusual to ignore. Wouldn't you like to read about some of them?

206 Do we have any alien-looking plants on Earth?

Sci-fi movies have always been a popular choice with the youth. There is something about watching things that are beyond ones imagination that makes us want to look at the weird and unusual things in films. However, art is often inspired by life. There is an island named Socotra in Yemen. This place is so cut off from the mainland that the plant life that has flourished on it is entirely unique. This island has given birth to some of the most alien-looking plants, and is known as the 'Most alien-looking place on Earth.' Take a look, doesn't it look like something out of the movie Avatar?

207 What is the Da Vinci's Rule of the Trees?

Who doesn't know the Mona Lisa and its famous creator, Leonardo Da Vinci? If some of the recent literature is to be believed, he was also a major contributor to the sciences. His diagrams on flying machines have been the inspiration of many airborne vehicles that we have today. But Da Vinci also had multiple theories and rules in other fields of science, namely, botany. Da Vinci came up with a rule for trees. According to it, the total girth of all the branches on a tree is equal to the girth of the trunk of the tree. Notice any tree in your vicinity. What do you think?

208 Why do ancient trees need protection?

A country's government sometimes cordons off or adds protection to monuments of historical relevance. Did you know that this is also true of natural monuments like rock structures and trees? There are trees on our planet that are thousands of years old! These trees are as good as biological pyramids. However, everyone does not appreciate the historical status given to these trees, and so the government, or a historical institution needs to step in to ensure that the trees are protected. If you don't believe trees need protecting, then know that an addict in Florida ended up setting fire to a 3500 tree when he was hiding inside it!

209 Are there any ancient tree houses ?

Living on top of trees would be an excellent way of staying out of reach of any land-bound predators. Although, there are no ancient tree houses available for us to take a look at, entire cities are known to have been built on top of tree trunks. An example is the beautiful islands of Venice, Italy. The central part of Venice still stands on tree trunks for almost 1200 years! You might wonder how these trunks haven't rotted yet considering that they are submerged in water. But you'd be surprised to know that these trunks have hardened as the water they came in contact with is rich in minerals that caused the trunks to harden. It is anticipated that in about thousand years, the trunks will have so much minerals that they will become rock solid and will begin to look like stone pillars!

210 Which is the world's oldest and tallest tree ?

When it comes to nature, humans have a tendency of leaving a disaster in their wake. Is it then really a surprise that nature needs to be protected? Can you imagine what would happen if there was an oldest and tallest tree that was open to the public? We'd all go to see it! There would be so many people from all over the world who would put it on their list of things to see. How do you think this would affect the growth of the tree? We can only imagine the damage caused to the natural surrounding of the tree, not to forget the tree itself with so many people wanting to commemorate their visit by carving their names into it! This is why, the world's tallest and oldest trees are kept top secret. This information is not publicly available mainly to protect the trees.

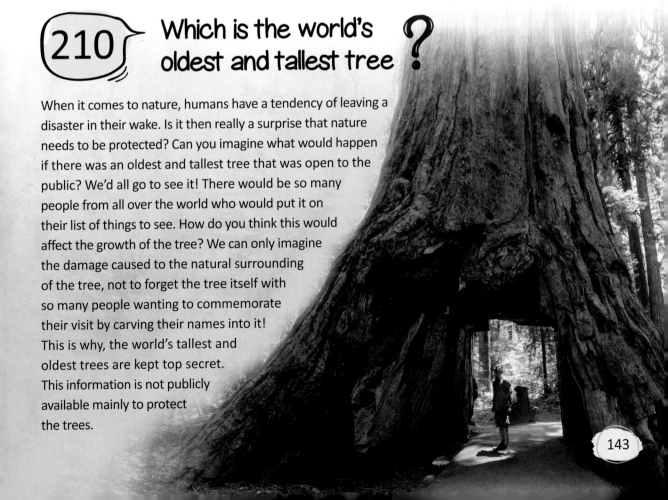

211 What is the baseball plant ?

Doesn't the name of this plant bring to mind a plant
with baseballs hanging from it? If only baseballs
grew on trees. If you lost one, you could simply pluck
another one off the plant! Well, if you were wishing
for one, take a look at the baseball plant, also known
as, *euphorbia obesa*. This plant grows in South Africa.
By itself, it grows up to 20 cm tall and produces fruits
that are exactly the size of baseballs. These plants are
also extremely rare and so are under protection by the
National Nature Conservation. Besides they are toxic.

212 Which is the most poisonous tree known to man ?

We all know that there are certain trees or plants that are quite harmful to you if ingested,
or if they come in contact with exposed skin. But did you know that there is a plant that is
so poisonous that if it rains and the rainwater from the leaves fall on you, they can cause
blindness. If the tree is on fire, the smoke is fatal. Any part of it coming in contact with
water can render the water poisonous for human consumption! This is the Machineel tree
that is found in Florida. Nature sure can fight back.

213 Is it possible to own a tree ?

Wouldn't it be nice if there was a tree out there that belonged to you? You could plant them and reap their fruit, maybe even build a tree house on it. Unfortunately, it is not possible to own a tree unless you own the land that it stands on. That is why farmers and orchard owners have very strictly-marked borders and fences. Even if you were to plant a tree in someone else's property and water it for years, the tree would still legally belong to the landowner. However, there is a tree in Athens, Georgia that is owned by itself! The owner, Professor Jackson loved the oak tree so much that he willed the tree and 8 square feet of the land around it to the tree itself.

214 Can trees recognise other trees around them ?

One would think that only humans could come up with something as selfish and mean as the concept of discrimination. But would it be really unbelievable if discrimination existed in nature itself? When a group of trees or plants are planted in the same soil, they compete for nutrients in the soil. The smallest plants end up withering owing to the survival of the fittest. However, it has been found that trees of the same species will end up helping each other out. Like a bigger tree will end up sharing its nutrients with a smaller one of the same species.

(215) Are the barks of trees always brown ?

If there is one thing we know about Mother Nature, it is that she loves colours. Leaves, flowers, grass, animals are found in all colours, shapes and sizes. If we were to observe a tree, it has leaves, flowers, fruits and a chunky brown bark. The bark is usually a shade of brown ranging from beige to blackish-brown with variations of red. But did you know that there is a tree in Hawaii which has a multi-coloured bark? The Eucalyptus tree of Hawaii has rainbow colours naturally in it. Looks like Mother Nature liked this tree a lot!

(216) Why is the bark of a tree so hard ?

You can pluck flowers and fruits off a tree quite easily. Even some branches are soft and flexible and can be broken by a strong wind. But the bark of the tree is relatively strong and immovable. Why so? The bark is hard, because it is made up of 99 per cent dead cells. Of the entire tree only 1 per cent of an average tree has living cells in it. These cells are concentrated in the leaves, the tips of the roots and the layer of cells under the bark of the tree. Phloem consists of living cells that help transfer food from the leaves to the other parts of the plant.

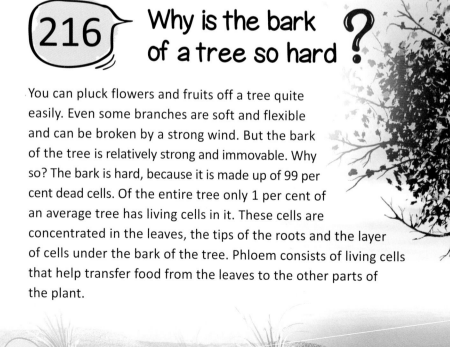

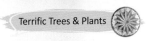

217 Is it possible to create a new forest ?

If humans can cut down trees and destroy whole forests at one go, planting them is possible as well. However, this would take a lot of work and time, as well as effort towards caring for the plants. The amount of money such a project would cost is a different story altogether. Although seemingly impossible, such a task has been undertaken and followed through by Jadav Molai Payeng. Payeng, from India, was 16 when he planted his first tree and has been planting trees ever since. He chose a barren sandbar to plant thousands of tree. Today, this place is a jungle that expands to 1360 acres! Wild animals like tigers, elephants and so on, live here.

218 Are there trees with eyes ?

What a scary image to have! Can you imagine a tree with eyes staring back at you from its branches? Well if you can't imagine it then take a look at the baneberry plant. This plant, also known as *Actaea pachypoda* has little spherical fruits. These fruits are white with a black dot at the centre, making them look like creepy eyeballs hanging from its branches. The fruits are about 6 mm small and are poisonous. So if you were to find one, do not eat it. However, you could try to plant one in your lawn during Halloween. It would work perfectly, to scare off the neighbour's kids!

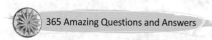

219   What is the bleeding tooth fungus ❓

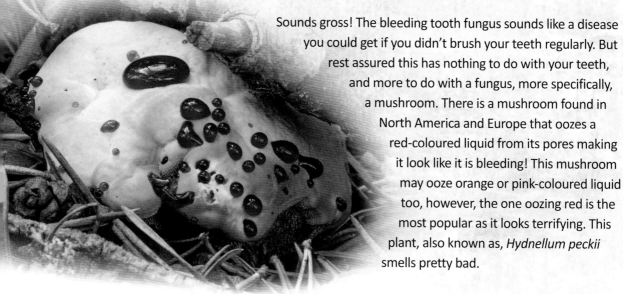

Sounds gross! The bleeding tooth fungus sounds like a disease you could get if you didn't brush your teeth regularly. But rest assured this has nothing to do with your teeth, and more to do with a fungus, more specifically, a mushroom. There is a mushroom found in North America and Europe that oozes a red-coloured liquid from its pores making it look like it is bleeding! This mushroom may ooze orange or pink-coloured liquid too, however, the one oozing red is the most popular as it looks terrifying. This plant, also known as, *Hydnellum peckii* smells pretty bad.

220   What unique plant is found in Namibian deserts ❓

The *Welwitschia mirabilis* is a plant found in the sandy deserts of Namibia. This plant is unique because unlike other trees that have many leaves, it has only two leaves and, no stem or bark! These two leaves are very long and over a period of time may tear or shred to look like weed. However, the whole mass originates from two leaves only. The plant is so strong that it can live in extreme desert conditions for 500 – 1500 years! That's one tough plant, if you ask me.

221 What is the largest flower in the world ?

Have you ever wondered how convenient it would be if you could pluck only one large flower as a gift for someone rather than plucking multiple flowers to create a bouquet? How about if there was a flower that was over 3 feet big? The world's largest flower is not only unique by its size, but also by its name. It is called the Corpse flower! The Corpse flower looks like a huge wilted wooden flower. Also known as the *Titan Arum*, this flower has a really bad stench. It blooms only once every 40 years and is so rare that it is protected by law!

That's a Stat!

Today the beautiful fragrance of the lavender flower is used in a variety of products like soap, creams, shampoos even potpourris. But in the past, lavender was used to treat a variety of ailments like headache, cholera and even the plague!

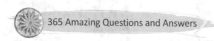

222 Can plants grow on stones ?

It is possible for a plant to grow on a stone as long as its roots can reach the soil and continue providing nutrition to the plant. The thing with stone is that it doesn't retain water, nor does it hold minerals, so if you were to leave a seed on top of a stone and water it daily, it may germinate, but unless its tiny roots can find soil, the plant will wilt away. However, if you are still interested in plants on stones, look up the Lithop. This plant has a green stem, but it has two leaves that have the colour, shape, and the look of stones! This strange species of plant is found in South Africa, and can live for up to 50 years.

223 What is the plant that moves when touched ?

You must have read about this plant in your science text books when studying about responsiveness to stimuli. However, since we are talking about strange plants, we cannot go ahead without including the popular Mimosa plant. Mimosa pudica is a plant that has compound leaves that close when touched. This is rarely seen in other plants. They have a water system that balances itself when a foreign body touches the leaves, causing it to close. After a while, when the leaves are left undisturbed, the water flow corrects itself, and the leaves open up again.

224 Which is the smallest plant in the world ?

The Wolffia species is known as the smallest flowering plant in the world. You must wonder, how small is this plant? Well, pick up your ruler. Do you see the 1 mm mark? Two full-grown Wolffia plants can fit inside that 0 – 1 mm mark! That is how small it is! Also known as duckweed, the Wolffia plant reproduces very fast. Some of these plants have a tiny flower on top of it. Did you know that some types of Wolffia can be eaten as well? An Asian variety of this plant is edible and quite nutritious as it is rich in protein!

225 Which plant has the largest floating leaf ?

All of us have seen some cartoon or the other where a small animal uses a lily pad to row itself across a lake or some form of water body. Wouldn't it be amazing if there was a lily pad big enough to support the weight of a human? Well, why not, as long as you weigh less than 40-45 kg? The *Victoria Amazonica* is a lily pad that grows up to 3 feet wide. The edges of this leaf folds upwards so that it doesn't overlap with other leaves, and the bottom of the leaves are prickly protecting it from being eaten. These plants also produce huge lilies that bloom only at night.

226 What are bladderworts ?

Bladderworts are carnivorous plants. If you look at the picture, they look quite ordinary with nothing vicious about them. But there are two interesting things about this plant. Firstly, it uses pockets of air to float on the surface of water bodies during the mating season. It gets rid of them when it is time to sink to the bottom of the same water body once the blooming period is over. And secondly, they trap small water animals by sucking them up! No trap, no scent to lure the prey into its trap, but a nature made vacuum hose that pulls even small fish into the body of the plant that ingests it!

227 How does the African Acacia tree protect itself ?

You may have seen this tree on many wallpapers and calendars. It is almost representative of the Savannah. This wise, seemingly innocent tree, however, holds a terrible secret. It is a murderer! There are herbivorous animals that feed on the leaves of this tree. When an animal approaches an Acacia it emits a gas in the air that warns all the other Acacia trees in the vicinity. These trees then begin to produce extra tannin in their leaves, which end up poisoning the poor animals that feed on it! All that glitters is not gold and all that's green is not healthy!

228 Which is the world's largest single stem tree?

Do you remember seeing a banyan tree with its roots hanging from the branches? It seems like the biggest tree ever! However there are bigger trees than that, and the biggest in the world is the 'General Sherman' which is a Giant Sequoia. When you say the biggest tree, it is not the tallest or the broadest; it simply is the biggest single tree in the world at 275 feet tall, and as broad as a bus!

GENERAL SHERMAN

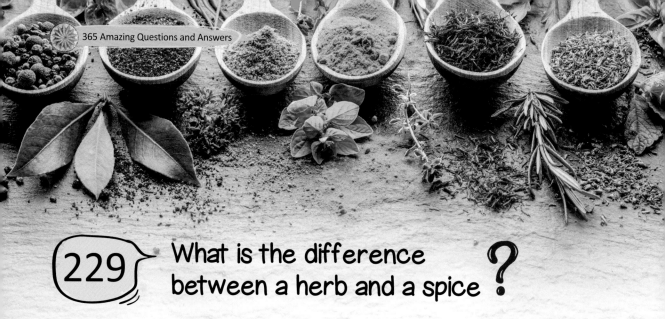

229 What is the difference between a herb and a spice ?

If you have ever given your mother a helping hand in the kitchen, you would have noticed that she has a variety of little bottles. Some hold spices and others hold dried herbs. Why not call them all spices? Why the classification? The reason for this is simple. The herbs that you see bottled in the kitchen are taken from the leaf of a plant (usually a herb), while the spices come from everything else of a plant, like the seed, berry, stem, bark, root or bulb. Hence, basil, oregano, mint, parsley are herbs while, cardamom, cinnamon, nutmeg and cumin are spices.

230 Which tree covers the maximum area ?

The Aspen of Southern Utah would appear like the woods to you. It is almost like a jungle full of narrow trees, known as the Pando tree. A single tree wouldn't be able to cast sufficient shade to protect one person. Then how does it qualify to be the tree covering the maximum area? Simple, dig a bit deeper, literally! Take a look at the roots. All the trees spread over 106 acres of land share the same root system. Their roots, are all connected to each other. This makes all the 40,000 trees qualify as a single tree! And hence, it bags the award for the tree that covers the maximum area.

231 What is the natural use of caffeine?

Surely Mother Nature could not have predicted that humans would reach a point in life when they would need help just waking up in the morning! But thank God for coffee, anyway. Then how did caffeine come to be? Well, like most of the other naturally occurring substances, humans simply saw something useful in nature and started using it. Caffeine in coffee bean plants is a form of in-built

insecticide. It helps the plants get rid of insects and pests, and keeps them from feeding on the leaves and seeds. This naturally occurring poison became sweet nectar for us. As they say, one man's trash is another man's treasure.

232 Have any extinct plants ever been revived?

A plant may become extinct if its entire living species has perished and there is no part or living cells of the plant available, to enable a new plant to grow. However, we do have botanists, specialists and experts who work hard day and night to replicate the DNA of these plants or to artificially create these plants. As you know, Mother Nature is not easy to copy. There was a flowering plant that had gone extinct, but scientists found the fruit of this plant. The fruit was in the stomach of a squirrel that had been preserved in ice about 32,000 years ago! Scientists were able to bring this extinct plant belonging to the species *Silene stenophylla* back to life.

233 — Why are figs not an appropriate vegan option?

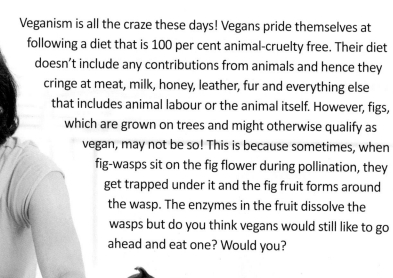

Veganism is all the craze these days! Vegans pride themselves at following a diet that is 100 per cent animal-cruelty free. Their diet doesn't include any contributions from animals and hence they cringe at meat, milk, honey, leather, fur and everything else that includes animal labour or the animal itself. However, figs, which are grown on trees and might otherwise qualify as vegan, may not be so! This is because sometimes, when fig-wasps sit on the fig flower during pollination, they get trapped under it and the fig fruit forms around the wasp. The enzymes in the fruit dissolve the wasps but do you think vegans would still like to go ahead and eat one? Would you?

234 — What is the connection between corn, beans and squash?

You may have heard of a crop cycle. Farmers plant a certain crop at a certain time of the year and then follow it with another plant. They keep alternating these crops throughout the year. In this way they get the maximum benefit out of the soil. However, there are certain crops that work best when planted together. Corn, beans and squash work that way. The corn crop grows tall and has a structure. Planting it with the beans allows the soft bean stem to use the corn crop for support, encouraging its growth and exposure to the Sun. Beans on the other hand are rich in nitrogen that helps nourish the corn crop. And the squash vines that cover the soil ensures that weeds never grow, and there is no competition for the nutrients in the soil. It is a complete symbiosis.

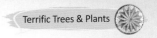

235 Why is the lotus considered to be sacred ?

Many civilisations consider the Lotus flower to be sacred. The Egyptians used this flower while performing their burial rites. In India, this flower is a symbol of purity and so is offered to God. All flowers are pretty and beautiful then why does the lotus hold the status of being sacred? It seems that this is one of the very few flowers that grows in mud. The flower has a long stalk that attaches itself to the bottom of a small water body. However, in order for the flower to survive, the water cannot be flowing, and stagnant water is bound to turn murky. But the flower has adapted to its surrounding, and its leaves have a wax coating which keeps the dirt from sticking to the flower. It is the only flower to maintain its cleanliness in dirt and is hence considered pure and sacred.

236 Which is the fastest growing plant?

Planting trees is a game of patience. If you were to plant a mango sapling it would take years before the sapling grows into a tree and produces any fruit for you. If you plant a seed, it is at least a day or two before a shoot pops out of the ground and that too, only if you watered it regularly. However, the bamboo plant is the fastest growing plant in the entire plant kingdom. Under favourable conditions, it can grow up to 3 feet everyday! So if you don't have the patience when it comes to gardening, plant a bamboo plant.

237 Where does vanilla extract come from?

Don't we all simply love the aroma that wafts out of a bakery? Cake tastes amazing, but a hot cake out of an oven smells heavenly, doesn't it? This aroma is often thanks to vanilla flavouring. Vanilla extract comes from a flower called *Vanilla planifolia*. This is a form of orchid and the vanilla extract is taken from its pods. These pods are called vanilla beans. Although they are called beans, they are not very closely related to the green beans family. They are closer to your common corn. *Vanilla planifolia* is one orchid whose smell can make your stomach rumble!

238 How did the pineapple get its name ?

There are a variety of fruits that we eat, like apples, bananas, strawberries, etc. But have you ever wondered about the pineapple? Seems like a strange name for a nice tropical fruit, doesn't it? The name combines two objects – pine and apple. This is so, because explorers who found pineapples thought that they resembled these two objects. The outer covering of the fruit was quite like a pinecone while the inner fruit was fleshy like an apple. And that is how the fruit came to be known as a pineapple!

239 Why are thistles prickly ?

Have you ever looked at a plant and wondered why it was that way? For example, little cactus pots look very cute on your windowsill but can still hurt a lot if you get too cosy around them. But just like the thorns on a cactus serve a purpose, the prickly leaves of thistles have a use too. They keep other animals from eating them. It is a way of self-preservation. These prickly plants have also earned their place in history. When the Vikings attacked the Scottish in the 13th century, the thistles proved to be extremely useful. They allowed the Scottish to escape while the Vikings were left making their way through painful thistle thorns. No wonder it is the National Flower of Scotland!

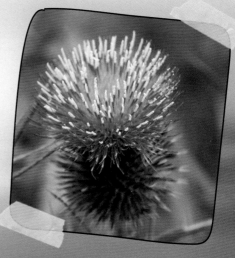

240 — Are plants sometimes named after Gods and Goddess ?

We have seen little boys and girls named after the Gods or saints that their parents worship. Hence we have names like Juno, Jupiter, Nicholas, so on and so forth. Similarly, we have botanists who would discover a new species of flower and instead of naming them using their own names would rather tribute it to one of the Gods. Hence we have Iris, who is the Greek Goddess of rainbows. Also, there is the milkweed whose scientific name is Asclepias, named after Greek God Asclepius, while the Hebe was also named after the Greek Goddess with the same name.

ASCLEPIAS

241 — What are the origins of the Aster flower ?

Many flowers are named after Gods and Goddesses. However, Aster is a Latin word for "star." There is a mythological story behind the existence of the Aster flower. It seems that the Greek Goddess Virgo was sad because there were not enough stars in the sky. This caused her so much despair that she wept and her tears fell to the Earth. According to mythology, when the tears touched the soil, they turned into Aster flowers. These flowers are considered to be divine, and since then they have been offered to the Gods. Some people also believe that after sunset when the flowers close, fairies sleep under their petals.

(242) Why do banyan trees have roots hanging from their branches?

Imagine that you are standing on a high stool. What would happen if you felt like you were losing your balance? You would immediately bend your knees and throw out your arms to regain your equilibrium, or find something to hold onto to steady yourself. The banyan trees are the same. They have a strong root system under them, however, they tend to grow so big and their branches extend to such a length that it might be possible for a strong wind to uproot them. So the tree adapted. The aerial roots that hang from its branches grow long enough to penetrate the ground reinforcing the root system and enabling it to stay steady come rain or storm.

243 Why are foxgloves called so ?

Have you ever heard of or seen the foxglove flower? It is a pretty, long, bell-shaped flower in shades of white and pink. If you don't find the name cute enough, imagine a fox wearing these flowers as gloves. The shape of the flower is quite compliant with the idea. But don't fall for the prettiness of these flowers, as each and every part of this plant is poisonous. Even inhaling dried pollen grains of this flower can result in a trip to the doctor. As for the name, the flowers are called foxgloves because, centuries ago, people actually believed that foxes slipped their feet in the leaves of this plant to silently stalk their prey.

244 What is arrowroot ?

Considering how some of the plants in the plant kingdom have been named, it would be no surprise if one believed that an arrowroot plant has roots shaped like arrows. The arrowroot, which is native to India, and scientifically known as *Maranta arundinacea*, is used as a replacement in cooking when working on a low-carb diet. It is used as a thickening agent. However, it got its name from the fact that the powdered form of this root was used in the old days to treat arrow wounds. These arrows were dipped in poison, and the root powder was used to absorb the poison from the wound. It has saved many lives.

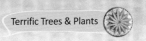

245 How can flowers be used to communicate?

Gifting flowers has been an age-old tradition. These days, the messages behind giving someone flowers are simplified.

A red rose stands for love, while a yellow one denotes friendship. A white flower is given to someone you have quarrelled with to initiate a truce, while a black/purple flower denotes enmity. However, in the Victorian times, the messages were quite different and meant a myriad of things. For example, a pink carnation would stand for "You are unforgettable," while a striped carnation would be a negative answer to a proposal. A purple hyacinth meant an apology, while a yellow one denoted jealousy. Beats texting doesn't it?

246 What is amber?

Do you remember Jurassic Park, the movie? The scientists use the DNA of a dinosaur extracted from a mosquito that has been fossilised inside a blob of amber, to clone dinosaurs.

Some trees create a thick, clear, sticky liquid called resin. This resin has many uses. Humans have used it to make rubber, glue and even certain forms of plastic. When resin dries up trapping bits of tree bark or insects it hardens into a snow globe-like blob. This dried up resin is called amber. It is usually a transparent yellow-orangish colour and has a natural beauty of its own.

247 What is the speciality of aster leaves?

Different people have different ways of warding off evil. Some people hang blue charms with an eerie iris in the centre, some hang garlic garlands at their windows, others nail a tiny black rag doll to the main doors. However, some people burn aster leaves to ward off evil. The truth is that the smoke produced by the aster leaves irritated snakes and kept them away from residences. Over time, aster leaves came to be burnt to ward of evil in general.

248 Why are some roots edible?

When you picture a plant, you think of the green leaves, a sturdy stem, a couple of flowers and fruits and last of all, the roots. The roots are underground and so consuming something that has been buried in soil doesn't seem like a good idea. However, many plants store a lot of nutrition in their roots. And that is how we end up having edible roots like carrots, ginger and radish. The roots also tend to be more nutritious than the fruits as they are closer to the source of nutrition and absorb both vitamins and minerals directly from the soil. Roots are also a good source of fibre.

249 Can we eat flowers ?

Some flowers are indeed edible. Certain variations of begonias, carnations and even chrysanthemums are used as a part of salads, especially the leaves. Not only do they add a splash of brilliant colour to the salads but also a dash of taste that is peculiar to flowers. But did you know that there is a flower that you have been eating without realising it? Broccoli is actually a flower. If you were to allow a stem to grow, the little flowers at its ends would bloom into little yellow flowers! Cauliflowers are flowers too.

250 Which was the first plant to be cloned ?

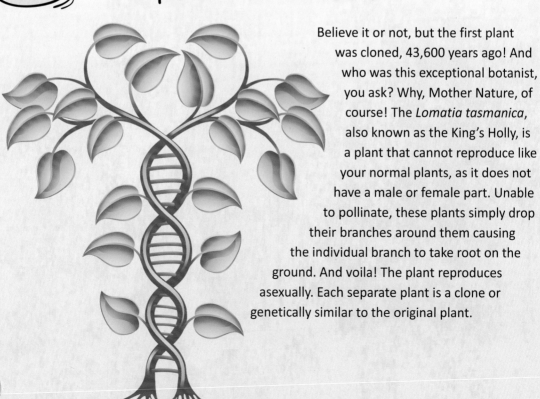

Believe it or not, but the first plant was cloned, 43,600 years ago! And who was this exceptional botanist, you ask? Why, Mother Nature, of course! The *Lomatia tasmanica*, also known as the King's Holly, is a plant that cannot reproduce like your normal plants, as it does not have a male or female part. Unable to pollinate, these plants simply drop their branches around them causing the individual branch to take root on the ground. And voila! The plant reproduces asexually. Each separate plant is a clone or genetically similar to the original plant.

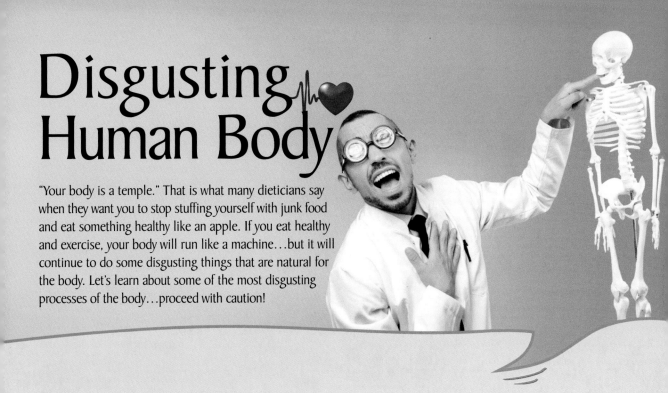

Disgusting Human Body

"Your body is a temple." That is what many dieticians say when they want you to stop stuffing yourself with junk food and eat something healthy like an apple. If you eat healthy and exercise, your body will run like a machine…but it will continue to do some disgusting things that are natural for the body. Let's learn about some of the most disgusting processes of the body…proceed with caution!

251 Can you tickle yourself?

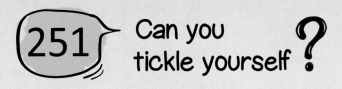

No. Try it. You cannot tickle yourself. This doesn't mean that you can't do the action. It means that it won't have the same giggly effect that it will have when you tickle a friend or sibling. So why can't you tickle yourself? It's all in the brain.

The brain knows what to feel in reaction to something. When someone tickles you, even if they give plenty of warning beforehand, you laugh out of a feeling of nervousness, as your brain associates tickling with spiders or other crawly insects climbing on you. However, when you tickle yourself, this sensation is absent so it doesn't work.

252 Does your stomach blush ?

Sometimes you might feel warm all over your body, especially your stomach, when you blush. Well, it could be because your stomach is blushing along with you. Actually, your stomach lining is 'turning red' just like your cheeks. Remember, the human stomach is a muscle that expands and contracts.

When you blush, your sympathetic nervous system sends a signal to your body to increase the blood flow. And when you are embarrassed, the body releases adrenaline which makes the blood vessels dilate so that the blood flow and oxygen delivery is improved. That's when you blush, because the veins in your face have more blood flowing through them. Your stomach lining appears red for the same reason.

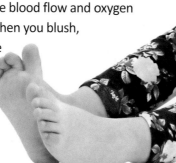

253 Why doesn't the stomach digest itself ?

Our stomach is protected because of the epithelial cells. These cells make and release a solution that coats the mucosa which is the inner layer of the stomach. The inner layer is made up of specialised cells like g-cells and epithelial cells.

This solution is called bicarbonate and is highly alkaline. If you know your acids and bases, you'd know that this alkali can neutralise the acid released by the parietal cells thus producing water and saving us. If the epithelial cells ever stops producing this bicarbonate, then the stomach will begin to auto digest, which means it will digest itself as there is more acid and nothing to neutralise it.

254 Can bacteria live in the stomach?

Yes they can! Bacteria live in the digestive tracts. They are nicknamed the 'gut bacteria'. There are trillions of bacteria that live in our body, most of them have settled in the digestive tract to break down the food we eat. They even absorb nutrients. They could also affect weight loss, inflammation and mood swings.

They could control the insulin activity as well and control how the body reacts to carbohydrates. 'Good bacteria' like probiotics increase how long we live. The healthier the stomach, the happier the mind. So, even if the idea of bacteria in the stomach grosses you out, remember they are there for a reason!

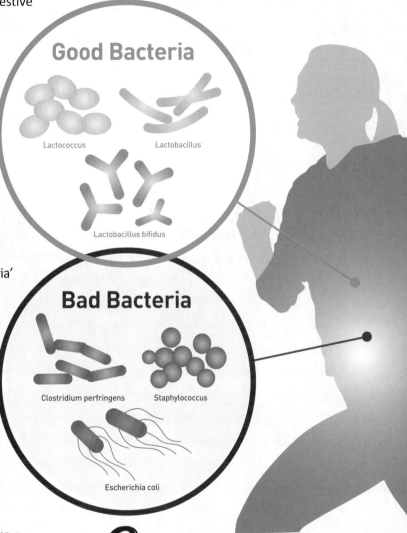

Good Bacteria

Lactococcus

Lactobacillus

Lactobacillus bifidus

Bad Bacteria

Clostridium perfringens

Staphylococcus

Escherichia coli

255 Are there harmful bacteria?

Yes! You've just read about some friendly bacteria that live in the stomach. But don't get too happy. There are some bacteria that are waiting for human beings to die to get to work decomposing the bodies. All human beings have bacteria inside them, and outside, on their skin. They are in the air, water and on everything. There's no way of seeing them to know what they are up to!

You know the friendly bacteria in the stomach. They begin the decomposing process from the inside. The bacteria on the skin also start working immediately. The immune system and the body temperature are the only things that keep them at bay.

256 Can tumours grow teeth

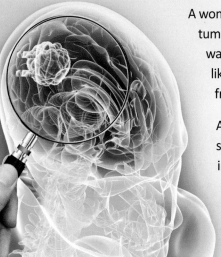

A woman named Yamini Karanam was diagnosed with a brain tumour. During a doctor's visit, she was told that her tumour was growing, a bone! It even began to grow what looked like hair and teeth. This is called a teratoma. It is translated from a Greek word called 'monstrous tumour'.

Apparently, when she was still in her mother's stomach, some tissue erroneously broke away and folded up into the tube that was meant to become her brain. Statistically, this is what happens when abnormal growths are reported. Of 100 abnormal growths, 20 are teratomas. As freaky as they may seem, luckily, they can be cured with surgery. Which was good news for Yamini who was able to get it removed.

257 Why does day-old water taste funny ?

When you pour water into a glass, there are already some microorganisms in it. Once you put your lips to the glass to sip the water, new microorganisms are introduced from your mouth. Under the effect of the temperature of the room and the sunlight coming through the windows, the microorganisms could multiply fast.

That is why water tastes so funny when you keep it in a glass overnight. Left overnight, the microorganisms have doubled and tripled. Then your mouth microorganisms make it worse. It's still safe to drink. But, if you use dirty hands to hold the glass of water, the microorganisms from them can also get into the water.

258 Where do dead skin cells go?

You've heard of snakes who shed their skin and just leave it behind as they crawl away with a fresh, shiny coat of skin. But human beings shed dead skin cells regularly. Your skin is made of several layers. The first layer is the epidermis, which is the layer you can see. It's made up of keratin. The cells are called keratinocytes.

The layer after the epidermis is the dermis. The keratinocytes cells at the bottom of the epidermis form bonds with the dermis to form new cells. Just like climbing a mountain, the new cells push up to become the top layer. Their reward? Being destroyed by harsh weather and daily activities. That's when they slowly die off. When the cells die, they break off from the skin to allow new cells to push upwards.

This entire process takes one month. So, every month, we get a new top layer of cells. Imagine this process happening all over your body. That means that nearly 30,000 skin cells die off every hour and a million die off in a day.

Where do they go? Your dead skin cells mix with the dust that collects on everything around you.

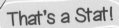

That's a Stat!

16 per cent of your body weight comes from your skin. There are 1.6 trillion skin cells in your body... imagine the dust!

259 Does everyone have a belly button ?

This is quite a rare sight, but there are some people who don't have a belly button. Why? It could be the result of a surgery performed during infancy to correct abdominal problems. It could also be because the baby was born with the internal muscles poking at the abdominal wall.

After birth, an infant might lose its belly button if the umbilical cord is left to dry and then drop off normally. Luckily, this is not the normal procedure around the world. It is normal to clamp and then cut the new-born baby's umbilical cord. In fact, this is what shapes the belly button!

260 Does your belly button clean itself ?

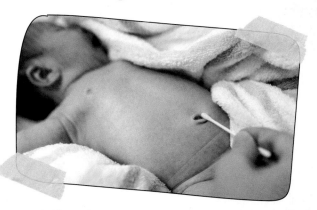

Your ears are self-cleaning. Your belly button is NOT! So, think about the last time you cleaned your belly button. If you don't clean your belly button regularly, then start now, because it is home to more than 60 different types of bacteria. Not only that, it's also where some of your moisturiser, lotion, cream and even food goes unnoticed. Soap flows into your belly button and dries up there as well.

Belly buttons also have dirt. This dirt can build up very quickly and eventually become visible. The layer of dirt in your belly button might be thin or thick depending on when you last cleaned it.

261 Does running make you poop?

Sometimes, runners feel a sudden urge to visit a toilet. A woman named Harrison Glotman was in the middle of a marathon when she suddenly realised that she must go to the toilet IMMEDIATELY.

New runners should get used to their bowel movements strangely making urgent demands. It's because running, and exercising in general, increases movement in the gastrointestinal tract. A runner's mobility increases because of exercise, which increases the mobility of this tract.

Our gastrointestinal tracts are made up of large muscles. Exercising increases the concentric contractions that move digested material to the intestines and then to the rectum. People who run long distances have improved circulation, which also affects the tract.

A runner's blood flow increases which means less blood goes to the gastrointestinal tract and stresses it. Runners feel better a few minutes after they run, because their blood supply is back to normal.

But running can also increase the chances of constipation. That's because the low blood supply to the gastrointestinal tract can make the body clam up. No matter the result, drinking a lot of water will help.

262 What's on your face ?

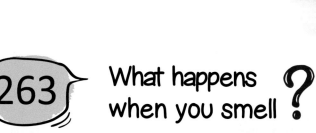

It hasn't been confirmed as yet, but you might have mites on your face. Tiny, microscopic, almost invisible mites who are happily eating, sleeping and crawling all over your face. It's not just some mites, nearly 48,000 species of mites could have made their home on your face. They travel to your hair and secrete some oil. That's why they are called 'face mites'.

They were first discovered, when a curious scientist pointed a microscope at some acne and noticed worm-like creatures crawling around there. Imagine, mites may even have gone to the moon with Neil Armstrong and come right back again!

263 What happens when you smell ?

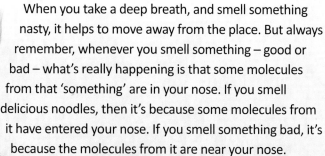

When you take a deep breath, and smell something nasty, it helps to move away from the place. But always remember, whenever you smell something – good or bad – what's really happening is that some molecules from that 'something' are in your nose. If you smell delicious noodles, then it's because some molecules from it have entered your nose. If you smell something bad, it's because the molecules from it are near your nose.

The molecules are light and easily evaporate. They float in the air and reach your nose. If you cannot smell something, it's because the molecules on that material (like steel) cannot evaporate. You can smell these molecules because they bind themselves to the hair-like structures called 'cilia' in your nasal passages.

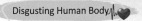

264 Can you eat metal ?

There are some strange people who eat razor blades and other small metal objects. They even eat pieces of glass and plastic bottles. This seems weird to people who like normal food. But can the stomach handle this?
Yes, but barely.

The stomach has a strong gastric acid made up of hydrochloric acid, potassium chloride and sodium chloride. The stomach acid digests and breaks up proteins. The stomach acid has a pH of 1 which is strong stuff.

Scientists have tested how metal corrodes when it encounters stomach acids in the laboratory. In a healthy stomach, a razor blade becomes soft and breaks in less than 24 hours. It's important to remember that a razor blade is made up of thin metal, but the effect of stomach acid on bigger, thicker metals is hard to test.

The stomach acid is so strong, but it doesn't dissolve the contents of the stomach. It definitely can. The stomach lining produces gastric acid. This lining is made of mucosal protein, which actually is like mucus, and coated with sugars that resist the effect of the acid...unless you have an ulcer.

265 Which body part does the baby first develop in the mother's womb ?

We all start off life as a single cell. In a little time, the single cell multiplies into many cells that slowly forms a ball of cells. This ball is hollow and attaches itself to the womb. Most of the cells in this ball becomes the embryo. The cells then form the different layers of the body.

The ectoderm which is the outer layer becomes the hair, nails and skin. The inner layer is the endoderm which becomes the intestines and lungs.

But before the head, heart and anything else is formed, the first part of the body that is formed is the anus. There are two types of embryos – one that develops in vertebrates like humans, dogs and cats. Others that develop in invertebrates like insects.

Basically, once the fertilised egg in the womb multiples its cells and forms that ball, it folds in on itself to form the gastrula which develops an opening at one end. The opening begins to pinch close which forms the anus.

266 What kind of cells do humans carry ?

Most of the 37.2 trillion cells in the human body are not human cells. They are bacterial cells. There are several colonies of bacteria living in or on our body. According to scientists, bacterial cells are present in far greater numbers than the human cells in our bodies. But they take up less space as compared to human cells, because they are smaller.

Bacterial cells begin to grow from birth, when babies take in bacteria from their mother's milk, skin and during birth. Then, as we eat, drink and travel, we take in more bacteria. The more we interact with other human beings, the more bacteria we take in.

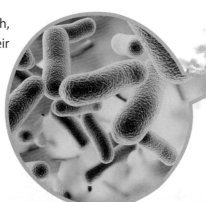

267 Which is the strongest muscle in the body ?

According to many people, the strongest muscle in your body might be the tongue while your jaw bone might be the hardest bone in your body. The belief that the tongue is the strongest muscle comes from the idea that it never gets tired or fatigued no matter how much you use it.

The tongue is said to be a strong muscle that is built with eight other muscles, each with the same task to perform. The tongue can repeat the same action several times without getting tired just by 'switching on' different muscles at different times. It does not form around a bone.

268 How much saliva do we produce?

During a lifetime, an average human being can produce nearly 23 kilolitres of saliva. This is enough saliva to fill two swimming pools. Every day, a human being produces about 75 ml to 1.5 l of saliva. While a person is sleeping, the production of saliva stops or comes very close to zero. But why do we produce so much saliva? What is its use? Saliva is the liquid that forms in the mouths of most living beings, including animals like dogs and lions.

About 99 per cent of saliva is water. It is produced by the salivary glands. Saliva also contains mucus, electrolytes and other substances that make it taste, feel and look much different from regular water. The main use of saliva is to protect the mouth from germs. So, even if you wake up in the morning with a mouth full of saliva and feel gross, remember that it is doing its job.

269 What organs can you survive without **?**

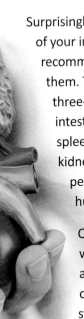

Surprisingly, you can survive without many of your internal organs. But, it's not recommended that you try to live without them. The body can adapt if it is missing three-fourth of the liver, most of the intestines, stomach, appendix, tonsils and spleen. It can still survive with just one kidney and one lung. If the organs from the pelvic and groin area stop working, the human body can still survive.

Of course, if so many organs are not working a person wouldn't be deemed as healthy. He or she would have a lot of medical problems, but they would still survive. The danger is if the brain or heart stops working.

270 How much iron does our body have **?**

Apparently, your body has enough iron to make a nail that's about 3 inches in length. An average man has 4 grams of iron in his body, while an average woman has 3.5 grams of iron. Children have 3 grams of iron. This amount of iron might seem small, but it is spread across the body in tissues, bone marrow, muscles, blood proteins, enzymes, haemoglobin and plasma.

In fact, the highest amount of iron goes to the haemoglobin. It is only during pregnancy and growth that more iron is needed by the body. Otherwise, during one day, a person uses up 1.5 mg of iron. That is why it is important to eat food with iron.

271 Is it natural to lose hair?

Hair loss is pretty common in all hairy animals and human beings. An average person is said to lose about 60 to 100 hair every day. That's like a tiny ball of hair that collects in your drain. But it's difficult to notice hair loss if you have short hair. For people with longer hair, it's easy to spot but creates a panic. If you shed more hair than that, then it's time to look for some hair therapy.

Hair loss can be seasonal where many women report that they lose more hair in the summers than in the winters. But it could also be because people wash their hair more during the summer, because of the outside heat and sweat collecting in their hair. At the same time, if you wash your hair less frequently, then every time you wash your hair, you will notice more hair loss.

What can cause hair loss? Anything from the stress of everyday life, to a flu or even starting a new diet. But once your body gets adjusted to any change in routine, the hair loss will stop. Losing hair can also be genetic, in that your genes will determine how healthy your hair can be.

That's a Stat!

An average person has about 100,000 hair on the head and they lose 100 hair a day. That's nearly 40,000 hair a year.

272 Can a sneeze travel ?

Our sneeze can travel as far as 200 feet from us. It depends on how fast it's going. For an average person, a sneeze can travel at 100 mph. This discovery was made by curious minds at the Massachusetts Institute of Technology.

However, some people argue that the sneeze doesn't go that far. Instead, it only travels at 35 mph to land 17 feet away from you. This is still pretty far. It might be worse if a person has a cold or a sneezing fit. So, the next time someone reminds you to cover your mouth, thank them. And remind others to cover their mouths as well!

280 What are tonsil stones ?

You might have heard of kidney stones. But have you heard of tonsil stones? Painful and tough stones sometimes form in the tonsils in a condition called "Tonsillitis". The tonsils have many small areas where bacteria can collect. They can also trap dead cells or mucous. The debris collected in these areas hardens and calcifies to form little white stones.

This problem mostly occurs in people who have an inflammation in their tonsils. It can happen more than once. The stones are generally small and easy to remove. They cause bad breath and sore throat, as well as swelling and ear pain.

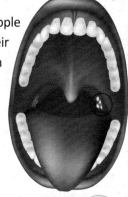

274 Are there different types of earwax ?

Yes! There actually are two different types of earwax. It's even determined genetically and according to your ethnicity. The two types are wet earwax, which appears yellow or dark brown and looks moist, and dry earwax which is grey and flaky and not very moist.

In the same way as curly hair comes from a recessive gene and straight hair comes from a dominant gene, wet earwax comes from a dominant gene while dry earwax comes from a recessive gene. Additionally, if you are an African or a European then you mostly have wet earwax. But if you are an Asian or a Native American, you might have dry earwax.

Ears are also self-cleaning. So, remember, removing earwax with the Q-tip is not recommended as it might harm your ears.

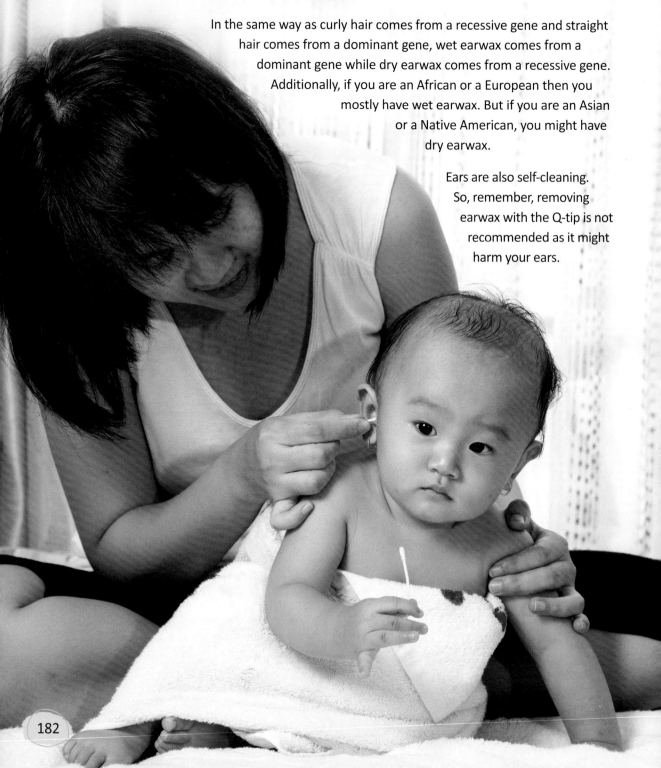

275 Do we swallow our mucous ?

It is very common to see small children pick their noses and consume the mucous. Some doctors believe that this strange habit probably builds the immune system. But they are against this bad habit as it could harm the nose to have a finger poking into it. Then again, they say that there is no need for us to try the mucous ourselves.

You naturally swallow about a litre of mucous every day. A man named Stefan Gates who is a British author, wrote a book titled *Gastronaut* where he says that our bodies are naturally built to eat it. The mucous that collects in the nose is swallowed after being moved inside by the cilia.

276 Do feet sweat ?

Absolutely! In fact, feet have nearly 500,000 sweat glands. They can produce half a litre of sweat every day. That is why it is not so surprising that our socks smell so much all the time. When feet sweat, it is quite normal. The sweat evaporates quickly. There are lots of bacteria on the feet. Even our hands and other parts of our body sweat.

Some people can have feet that smell excessively. They watch out for signs like itchiness, fungus, a bad smell, skin rashes, etc. That is why it is so important to maintain proper hygiene. Wash your feet regularly. Wear clean, fresh socks and wash your socks regularly. Wear comfortable shoes.

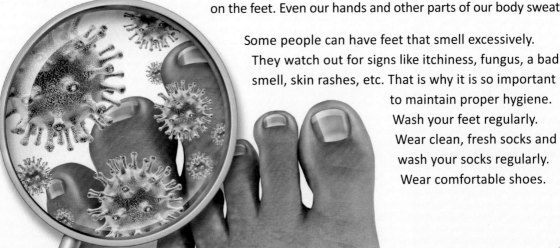

277 Can your eyes get bigger?

It's not hard to think that eyes don't grow from childhood to birth. Most babies have big eyes that look much too big for their face. On the other hand, their hands, feet, ears, nose and mouth all look much smaller than an adult's. A baby's eyes just look like a normal adult's eyes and equally big.

But eyes can in fact get bigger from childhood to adulthood. People have been researching this topic for a long time. To know if eyes grow, it's important to measure the eyeballs. Eyes grow the most during the first year of a child's life. They grow so fast that they need to slow down a bit for the other parts to catch up.

Imagine if a baby had adult's eyes? Then their eyes would be 1.5 times bigger than the ones you can see on a regular baby. So, why do babies have big eyes? It might even be to help them see better. A researcher once found that human beings can find things like big eyes, small noses and round faces cute. Everything that babies have!

278 Have you drunk dinosaur urine?

Everything about dinosaurs is fascinating. But what's disgusting is that it's possible, after all these years, we might be drinking dinosaur urine when we drink water. These are still unconfirmed claims from scientists and nothing is guaranteed. So, don't put down that glass of water just yet.

It's true that the amount of water on Earth has remained the same. The only change is that the water has moved on Earth many times. The dinosaurs remained on Earth for more than a century. That's why it's possible that every glass of water we drink has once passed through dinosaurs. In a hundred years, humans can say all the water they drank has passed through their human ancestors.

279 How clean is fresh urine?

It is commonly believed that urine is sterile. Some scientists claim that it is cleaner than saliva or the skin on your face. Urine, apparently, gets dirty as it leaves the body and comes in contact with bacteria, which unsterilizes it. This is just a theory, but it hasn't been proven.

Instead, recent studies show that urine is not sterile. Even healthy people have bacteria in their urine even before it leaves the body. The bacteria in the urine might be different and previously unidentified. However, even the new study has not determined the bacteria in the urine. Besides, there are other beneficial uses to urine.

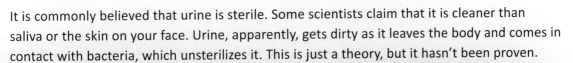

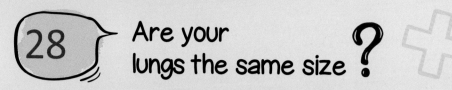

28 Are your lungs the same size?

No. The right lung is shorter and wider than the left lung so that there is sufficient space for the liver, which is right beneath the lungs. At the same time, the left lung is narrower than the right one so that the heart has enough space. The right lung actually has three sections called lobes while the left lung has two lobes. Each lung has a pleura sack. That is why even if one lung is punctured, the other continues to work and pick up the slack.

But together, the lungs occupy an area of 70 square metres. They have 2400 km of airways and 400 million hollow cavities. That's the size of a tennis court. Imagine if a person's lungs were opened and spread out, they would extend for 992 km.

A man's lung might be bigger than a woman's lung because they can hold more air. A man's lung can hold about 750 cubic centimetres of air at rest, while a woman's lung can hold 285 cubic centimetres of air at rest. And regardless of male or female, a person just uses up 70 per cent of the lung's total capacity in their life time.

Finally, lungs can protect themselves from harm. There are cilia on the bronchial tubes of the lung. These cilia, which are hair-like structures, sway back and forth constantly. They do this to spread mucus into the throat and get it out of the body. The mucus actually cleans the lungs and gets rid of the dust and germs trapped there.

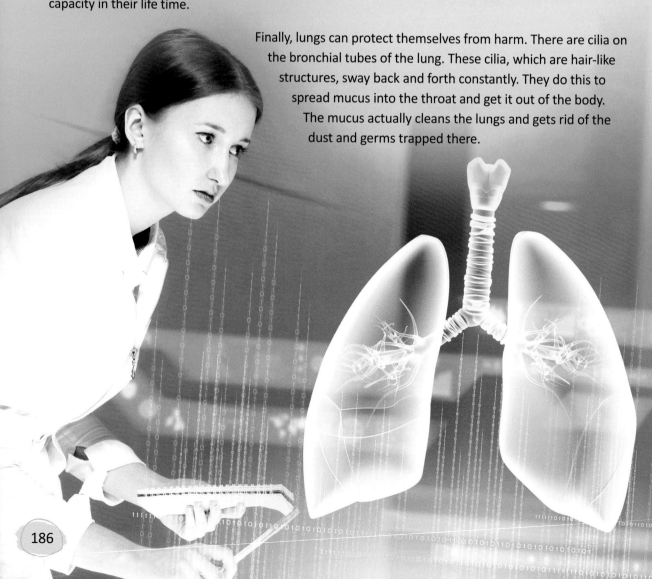

Culturally Speaking

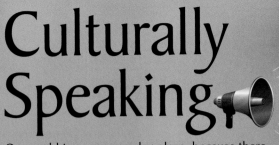

Our world is a very complex place, because there are so many different people in it. They eat different types of food and speak different languages like Hindi, English and Portuguese. Their clothes are often different and their beliefs, religions and practices are also different. Let us now read about different cultures.

281 How many people can speak English?

For many, English might not be their first language but they learn to speak it in school. English is considered an important language to move ahead in the world and work in a global economy. In 2006, a study showed that there are 400 million native English speakers and 400 million people for whom English is the second language.

Nearly, 700 million foreigners (people who live outside countries whose main language is English), chose to learn English. So, as an estimate, in 2015, you could say there are about 1.5 billion English speakers in the world. This number could only keep increasing as English is the official language of 67 countries.

282 What is a filler?

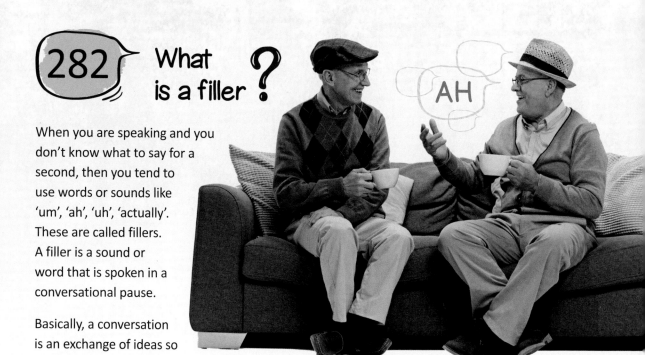

When you are speaking and you don't know what to say for a second, then you tend to use words or sounds like 'um', 'ah', 'uh', 'actually'. These are called fillers. A filler is a sound or word that is spoken in a conversational pause.

Basically, a conversation is an exchange of ideas so when one speaker finishes speaking, the other one jumps in immediately with their response or new idea. By using fillers, the current speaker is trying to indicate that he or she is not done speaking, just needs a second to think. In English, fillers are considered informal and you can't use them in papers or essays.

283 How many characters does the Chinese language use?

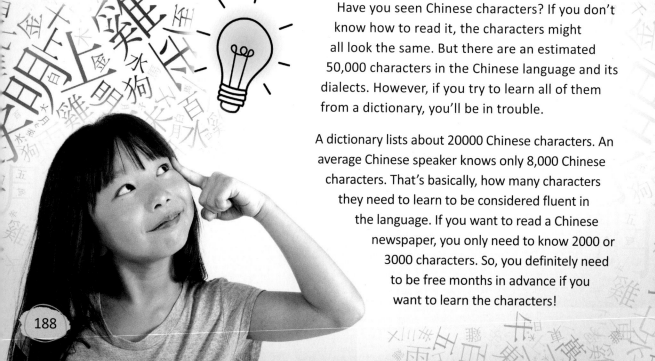

Have you seen Chinese characters? If you don't know how to read it, the characters might all look the same. But there are an estimated 50,000 characters in the Chinese language and its dialects. However, if you try to learn all of them from a dictionary, you'll be in trouble.

A dictionary lists about 20000 Chinese characters. An average Chinese speaker knows only 8,000 Chinese characters. That's basically, how many characters they need to learn to be considered fluent in the language. If you want to read a Chinese newspaper, you only need to know 2000 or 3000 characters. So, you definitely need to be free months in advance if you want to learn the characters!

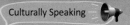

284 Can languages go extinct?

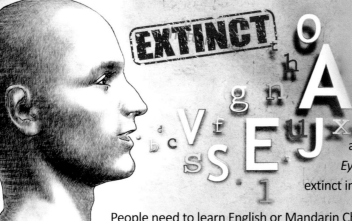

Yes! Apparently, languages are going extinct event faster than any plant or animal species. Every two weeks, a language goes extinct. The major culprit for this is economic development. It is a problem that affects the world. A language called *Eyak*, which was used in Alaska went extinct in 2008 when its only speaker died.

People need to learn English or Mandarin Chinese in order to get jobs or make progress at a global scale. They tend to ignore the lesser used languages and their own mother tongue to focus on learning these languages. There are very few people intervening to try and preserve extinct languages.

285 How many languages are there in the world?

The real number is not confirmed, but there are about 3000 to 8000 languages in the world. The big difference is because experts sometimes disagree about what is a language and what isn't. Some languages are like others but have some words or phrases that are different. Some languages are non-verbal, and it is difficult to tell if they are different from the non-verbal language from another region.

There are 845 million native Mandarin speakers which is the highest number for any language. Spanish and English occupy the second and third place respectively, while Hindi, Bengali and Portuguese occupy the next three places.

286 What is the official language of the US ?

English

The United States of America does not have an official language. This is surprising since most American people know and use the English language to communicate with each other. There are 67 countries who have declared English as their official language even though it is the second language for most of its citizens.

But declaring English as the official language is seen as 'Un-American' and unnecessary. In most countries, official languages are declared to indicate what language the government will use to write its laws. In the US, legislature is always introduced in English. Strangely, there are people in the US who oppose making English the official language.

287 Who was the first US President to greet people with a handshake ?

THOMAS JEFFERSON.

The US President George Washington would bow when dignitaries or important people visited to attend presidential receptions. The idea was to avoid all physical contact. Even President John Adams would bow. The bow was very formal with Washington holding a sword in one hand and a hat in the other. Apparently, Washington held these items to avoid a forced handshake.

Then, Thomas Jefferson began to greet people with handshakes and flipped the tradition on its head. Since then, all US presidents have shaken hands and hugged dignitaries. US President Bill Clinton convinced two enemies to shake hands to foster peace. More recently, President Barrack Obama began high-fiving famous guests to the White House.

288 Which are the three biggest celebrations in USA ?

The biggest celebration in the United States of America is Christmas. It is a religious holiday. Most Americans in USA are Christians and really get into the festivities. Even non-Christians celebrate Christmas with enthusiasm. It is not only a big religious festival but also has a wide commercial profit for shops and businesses.

Similarly, Thanksgiving, is widely celebrated in the US. It is another religious festival that is celebrated by the family. People take a few days off from work to celebrate the holidays. Following behind these two religious festivals is the Super Bowl. It is an American football sport event that's treated with equal enthusiasm to religious festivals.

289 How much pizza do Americans eat every day ?

Americans love pizza. So much so, that there are regular calculations made to check how much pizza Americans eat every day. In 2011, an organisation named the 'National Association of Pizza Operators' found that Americans were served about 100 acres of pizza every day.

The organisation's goal was to help create a feeling of community among small chain pizza operators. In fact, Americans ate a lot of pizzas and burgers that year, but turns out that they favoured the pizzas more than the burgers with Pizza Hut being their favourite pizza outlet of choice. The number has only increased over the years.

290 How many official languages does South Africa have?

II Languages

South Africa has eleven official languages. They are Afrikaans, English, Ndebele, Northern Sotho, Sotho, Swazi, Tsonga, Tswana, Venda, Xhosa and Zulu. These are the languages used by a majority of the population. Less than 2 per cent of the people in South Africa use a language outside this list. Most of them are bilingual and even multi-lingual.

Eight per cent of South African speakers have English as their mother tongue. But English is the official language that is used in the media, used by politicians to write rules and communicate speeches and also used in business. In fact, English is known by most urban speakers and is rare in the rural areas.

291 What is kosher?

'Kosher' is a standard or rating. It is a standard given to food, or a place where food is prepared that meets Jewish law. It describes the type of food that a Jewish person can eat. It also describes how the food must be prepared. Most practicing Jews look for places with the kosher certification when they want to eat outside.

According to kosher standards, meat and dairy products shouldn't be cooked together nor should they be eaten together. A third category refers to other food items that are neither meat nor dairy. Neutral food items are called 'pareve' which can be eaten with either dairy or meat.

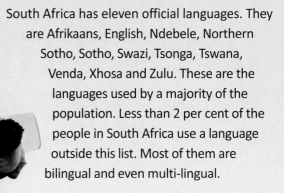

292 Do you put salt in your tea ?

It might seem unusual to you, but if you were living in Tibet, Mongolia or Western China, then sprinkling some salt in your tea or coffee would be a completely normal thing. They also add butter and milk.

Just like India, people in China like to drink savoury tea instead of the sweet tea that you normally see in European countries, specifically the United Kingdom. However, just a pinch of salt is added so it doesn't taste salty. In India, people have ginger tea which is another kind of savoury tea. Some people like to add salt in their coffee as surprisingly, the sprinkle of salt reduces the bitter taste of the coffee.

293 Is it illegal to sneeze ?

A place called Nebraska in the United States has several strange laws. One of these strange laws is that a person is not allowed to sneeze or burp while they are attending a church service. In fact, sneezing or burping is illegal in a church in Omaha, Nebraska.

The law is weird because people can't hold back sneezing or burping for long. They don't have full control over it. In Nebraska, it is also illegal to have fake teeth made of leather or for a mother to give her daughter a perm without state permission! So, if you ever feel like moving to Nebraska, make sure you read their laws carefully!

294 Which is the world's oldest country ?

San Marino is the world's oldest country. It is also one of the smallest countries in the world with an area of 60 km². It is a landlocked country. It has a bloody history of wars and invasion, but the citizens of this country have tried to keep their land intact. In fact, it is also one of the most beautiful places on Earth. Mount Titano is a part of the Apennine range, and it dominates the landscape of the country of San Marino. You can observe history and the effect of the wars fought here as there are three large fortresses on the sides of Titano's slopes.

San Marino is also considered to be the world's oldest republic and sovereign state. It was founded in 301 AD. The small size of the country helped to keep it safe, because neighbours and threatening forces did not take the country seriously, or as a threat. It earns a lot of its revenue from tourism as many people want to visit this beautiful country and learn its history. The stamps sold here are also keenly collected.

San Marino also has the world's oldest constitution, and it not only has no national debt, but its competent government is able to keep it out of a budget surplus. The country's life expectancy is the fifth highest in the world. And since it is so small and well-protected by its neighbours, it has no military forces.

295 What was used in place of money in Siberia ?

Before people began to use paper money, they used coins made of metals like gold, silver and bronze. And even before that, they traded goods and services to purchase things instead of using money. So, until the 19th century, tea bricks were exchanged by Siberians instead of money.

Tea bricks are blocks of ground black tea, green tea or other tea leaves. They are packed and moulded into blocks. Even though metallic coins were available at the time, tea bricks were the preferred form of 'currency' at the time. It is because tea could be drunk and even eaten. It was used in food items and as medicine to treat colds and coughs.

296 Which language do ATMs in the Vatican use ?

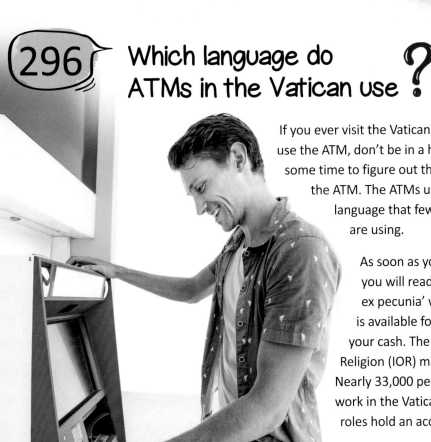

If you ever visit the Vatican City and need to use the ATM, don't be in a hurry. You will need some time to figure out the language used by the ATM. The ATMs use Latin, which is a language that fewer and fewer people are using.

As soon as you reach the ATM, you will read a line 'a deduction ex pecunia' which means that it is available for you to withdraw your cash. The Institute for Works of Religion (IOR) manages these ATMs. Nearly 33,000 people who live and work in the Vatican in various religious roles hold an account with them.

297 How many imaginary languages does The Lord of the Rings use ?

Many authors create imaginary languages or codes for their books. It enriches the reader's experience and helps them to create a universe that is separate from reality. That is why the author of *The Lord of the Rings*, J. R. R. Tolkein, created 14 imaginary languages in his books.

Of these languages, several are very popular. Some readers have become fluent in these languages as well. Often, imaginary languages are inspired by real languages that are either old or modern. Tolkein created new languages for hobbits, elves, wizards and other characters. Dwarvish, Quenya and Black Speech were some of the languages he created.

298 Which is the world's most translated book ?

The Bible is the world's most translated book! It has been translated into nearly 496 languages, these include the ancient languages like Hebrew, Sanskrit and Latin and also modern versions of languages like English and Hindi. The Bible has been translated into several Indian languages like Telugu, Tamil and Marathi.

The Bible is a book of religion for those who practice Christianity and Judaism. There are about 100 million copies of these books sold. Surprisingly, the second most translated book is *Pinocchio* and the most translated author is Agatha Christie. Right after *Pinocchio*, a book called *What does The Bible Really Teach* is the third most translated book. It has been translated into 244 languages.

HOLY BIBLE

299 How many imaginary languages are there in the world?

There are nearly 200 imaginary or artificial languages in the world. They have been invented by writers who wrote for television shows, radio shows, movies and books. Tolkein is the leading author on creating imaginary languages. But, artificial languages have gone as far back as ancient times when people invented languages to have philosophical debates.

The very first known artificial language was developed in the 17th century. At the time, there was a decline in the number of people speaking Latin in Europe. It was created because it was felt that the people of Europe needed to learn a new language for business and communication after their encounter with the Chinese.

300 Which language has the largest alphabet?

Khmer, which is a Cambodian language, has the largest alphabet in the world. It has 74 characters. It is an ancient script and the official language of Cambodia. The language has 16 million speakers. The language, like other languages, is influenced by Sanskrit and Pali which are also ancient languages.

There are 12 characters in the Rotokas language which is spoken in Papua New Guinea and uses the Latin writing system. Strangely, although Khmer has the most characters when compared to any other language, English has the most words. This maybe because it has so many speakers. New words are constantly coming up in the English language.

KHMER

301 Which country covers the most time zones

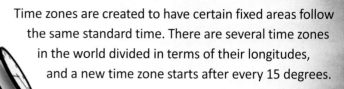

Time zones are created to have certain fixed areas follow the same standard time. There are several time zones in the world divided in terms of their longitudes, and a new time zone starts after every 15 degrees.

So, which country covers the most time zones? France! France also counts its overseas territories that it has laid claims to. It covers about 12 time zones, and the United States of America covers 11 time zones. On the other hand, Russia covers nine time zones. France's 12 time zones are spanned across French Polynesia, Marquesas Islands, Gambier Islands, Clipperton Islands, Saint Martin and surrounding areas, Metropolitan France etc.

302 Which is the least populated country ?

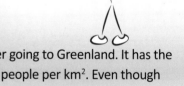

If you want to go to a quiet, isolated place for your next vacation, consider going to Greenland. It has the lowest population density in the world. It has a population density of 0.0 people per km². Even though Greenland is the largest island in the world it has a population of about 56,000 people.

The next least populated place in the world is the Falkland Islands with a population density of 0.3 people per km². It is an archipelago which lies on the Patagonian Shelf. It has a population of just about 3000 people. Mongolia, meanwhile, is the third least crowded country in the world with a population density of 1.9 people km².

303 Which country has the youngest population in the world?

Have you heard of the country of Niger? It has the youngest population in the world, which means typically people between the ages of 15 and 25. Surprisingly, low-income countries have younger populations. 70 per cent of Uganda's population is under 25, and almost 50 per cent is under 15. This country has the second youngest population in the world.

Mali and Malawi have the third and fourth youngest populations in the world. Albania has the highest percent of 15 to 24 year olds in Europe. On the same continent, Cyprus and Faroe Islands have a higher percent of 15 to 24 year olds. High-income countries have older populations. In countries where people live longer, there is a larger population momentum. On the other hand, African countries have the largest youth population in the world.

Antarctica, which has no permanent human population, has no young people. On the other hand, countries with the youngest population proportion are Guatemala, Haiti, Nicaragua. They have more people whose age is between 15 and 24 than those whose age is between 0 and 14. This is also true for Paraguay, Bolivia and Guyana.

304 What is Esperanto ?

Esperanto is a language that's made up entirely by a man named L. L. Zamenhof. He hadn't created the language for a book, like Tolkein, instead he wanted to unite people and stop having them waste time learning foreign languages. That's why, it's the most widely used artificial language in the world.

Zamenhof took 10 years to construct the artificial language and published a book teaching Esperanto grammar. Today, the language has 10 million speakers where about 1000 families are said to be native speakers with it as their first language. There are dialects like Ido derived from Esperanto. There are several other dialects as well.

305 Which country has the most lakes in the world ?

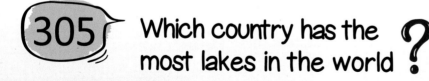

If you've visited Canada, then you probably already know that it has the most lakes in the world. There are nearly 3 million lakes in Canada. 60 per cent of these lakes, lie close to the borders of Canada, and only 9 per cent of them have freshwater.

Lake Huron, Lake Superior (which Canada shares with the US), the Great Bear Lake and Lake Erie are some of the important lakes of Canada. Canada has more lakes than all the countries in the world put together. But surprisingly, we know very little about these lakes and researchers are still trying to find information about them.

306 Why were cats hated in the Middle Ages ?

There is a big bias towards cats in the world. In India, people believe they should not cross a road. An owner with a lot of cats is observed sceptically. All of this might have a connection to the fact that female cat owners in the past were considered to be witches who could control people using magic.

Not only were women accused of being witches and burned, even cats were tortured by people in the Middle Ages in Europe. They had a bad reputation as people thought the devil transformed himself into a black cat and tricked people.

Middle Age writers claimed that cats chased mice as the devils chase souls and tried to further cement the links between cats and the devil. Even in the 20th century, a man named Walter Map wrote how devils first appeared as black cats before their cherished devotees. Witches were accused of shape shifting as black cats. None of this, of course, is true. But the bias stuck, and now many people around the world hate cats for no reason.

Cats are often portrayed as cunning and evil in literature. But luckily, in many places, cruel treatment of cats is banned and illegal and punishable by law.

That's a Stat!

There are many stray cats and dogs in the world. Around 60,000,000 cats live on the streets of USA. Most cats are found sleeping as cats like to sleep for 16 hours a day.

307 Who sells the most cheese ?

We don't exactly know which country can be credited with the invention of cheese, but France tops the list in terms of production and quality. There are about 350 to 450 types of cheeses found in France, and they are grouped into eight main categories. In this way, France has nearly 1000 unique types of cheeses that are original and derived.

Even a President of France was quoted saying, "How do you govern a country that has more than 250 types of cheeses?" Even the cheese production in France is unique and classified into four types – farmhouse, artisanal, cooperative and industrial.

308 Which is the most common surname ?

Most people have a last name Li or Lee. Next on the list are names like Zhang, Wang and Nguyen. Many of the last names sound Asian, because Asia has the highest population in the world. On the other hand, Garcia, Gonzalez and Hernandez are the next on the list, and they are all Latin last names. Smith, Smirnov and Miller are also a part of the list.

The three most common last names come from China, because it is the most populated country in the world. Nearly 100 million people in China, Korea and Vietnam have the surname Lee or Li. The name comes from the Chinese word for plum tree.

Name:
Sung Lee

309 Which country has the most overweight population ?

Nauru is a tiny country, but it is the most obese country in the world. Obesity is a problem around the world. About one in 10 people around the world are obese. That's about half a billion adults. Urbanisation, sedentary lifestyles and adopting western fast food has led to this rise in obesity.

The average person in Nauru has a body mass index of 34 to 35 and that's considered obese. It has a population of less than 10,000 people, yet since the country has imported fast food, it has seen a rise in obesity. Fried chicken and cola is the favourite food combination of the people of Nauru.

310 Why are most people of Luxembourg trilingual ?

Luxembourg's official language is Luxembourgish. On the other hand, they use French, German and Luxembourgish to conduct administrative and official work. So, if you were a child growing up in Luxembourg, you would spend a lot of your study time learning languages.

About 70 per cent of the population speaks Luxembourgish at work, school and even at home. But 55 and 30 per cent speak French and German at work and home respectively. Luxembourgish is the 'principal' language of 58 per cent of the population, which basically means it is their mother tongue. They even speak some Portuguese.

311 Which countries can disappear in the next 20 years ?

Global warming is getting worse every day. Each year seems to be hotter than the previous. Countries located closer to water bodies are experiencing more natural disasters. Maldives, an island state, is predicted to disappear within the next two decades after a giant tsunami hits it. The rising sea levels caused by global warming will be the culprit.

The President of Maldives has even begun looking to buy land from a neighbouring region to resettle and rehabilitate the people of Maldives. Guess he believes that prevention is better than cure. That's because many scientists have claimed that the Maldives sinking is not just a warning but an inevitability.

312 Which country's citizens have 167 sheep ?

The Falkland Islands in the United Kingdom has a small population of less than 3000 people. The sheep population of the Falkland Islands outnumbers the human population by a large number. There are half a million sheep in the Falkland Islands.

So, a permanent citizen of the Falkland Islands can easily get into sheep rearing. It is an odd ratio where each resident can have about 167 sheep compared to the seven sheep per person ratio of New Zealand. West Falkland has about 179,700 sheep while East Falkland has approximately 280,614 sheep. There are about 28,000 sheep in the smaller islands. If you are planning to move there, getting sweaters won't be a problem!

Can learning a second language increase your intelligence?

A polyglot is a person who knows and uses many languages. Becoming a polyglot is recommended by scientists as it is said to boost the brain power and also slow down the inevitable aging of the mind.

In fact, learning a second language is said to benefit the intelligence, memory power and concentration of a person. It also lowers the risk of getting Alzheimer's disease, because understanding a language is one of the toughest things that the brain can do. It requires understanding, learning, concentration and memory skills.

Studying a second or even a third language during ones childhood also keeps the brain active and helps it grow well. A long time ago, it was considered bad for a child to learn a second language as people believed putting children through such a strenuous mental workout would stunt their growth.

Being bilingual helps the cognitive skills of the brain and allows the brain to function properly. Compared to people who speak just one language, bilingual speakers have a greater intelligence, are better at planning and making decisions, they are better at math, reading and vocabulary and have a better grasp of their surroundings.

Learning another language also makes people feel empathy. They have greater mental flexibility and can switch easily between tasks. They are also more creative and have greater listening skills.

314 What's special about the postage stamps in Israel ?

The postage stamps in Israel are kosher. Kosher means they are made following specific standards of the Jewish religious law. That is because most of the population in Israel is Jewish. Kosher means dietary laws that handle food – especially meat and meat products.

ISRAEL Postage stamp

Lorem Ipsum

Lorem ipsum dolor sit amet, consectetur adipiscing elit, sed do eiusmod tempor incididunt ut labore et dolore magna aliqua. Ut enim ad minim veniam, quis nostrud exercitation ullamco laboris nisi ut aliquip ex ea commodo consequat.

Israel's Jewish population increased by 80 per cent since 1948. Since then, 60 per cent of the Jewish people have said that they follow kosher guidelines. Even the cows in Israel eat kosher food during the Jewish holiday of Passover.

They eat beans and hummus instead of grains. As a result, since so many people observe kosher standards in Israel, the postage stamps are also kosher.

315 Which place has no rivers ?

Saudi Arabia is a land where there are no permanent rivers. There is no flowing water constantly supplying its people with water for drinking and other purposes. It is a strange thing because Saudi Arabia is a huge country with a large population.

There are 17 such countries that don't have permanent rivers. Among them, Saudi Arabia is the largest followed by Oman, Qatar, Yemen, United Arab Emirates, Bahrain and Kuwait. They have some dry river beds and temporarily flowing water bodies during the monsoon season. Monaco and Vatican City are very small countries and sadly, no water body falls within their boundaries.

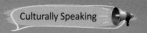

316 Which country's residents mostly live abroad ?

That's Malta, an island country! It is an archipelago in the Mediterranean Sea. Many residents of Malta travel abroad. In 2007 between January and July, it was calculated that around 152,326 people from Malta travelled abroad. There was a 11.4 per cent increase from 2006. The number of people who travel abroad is on the rise.

About 87 per cent of the Maltese population travelled to European countries or countries that belong to the European Union. The United Kingdom was the most popular destination out of all the European countries. There were more male passengers than female passengers. Of the total passengers that travelled abroad, 59.6 per cent were men.

Most of the passengers who travelled abroad were young and of ages between 25 and 44. About 46.5 per cent of the total travellers were of the younger demographic. The older population of age 46 to 64, accounted for 36.8 per cent of the total outbound travellers.

Most travellers liked to take direct air routes out of Malta. After the United Kingdom, about 30,080 people travelled to Italy. Most Maltese travelled looking for jobs. But once they received citizenship for other countries, they had to give up certain rights in their own country.

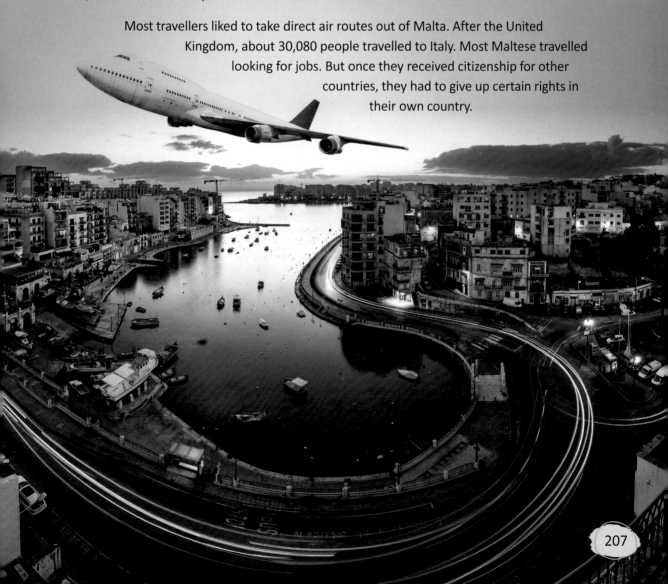

317 Where were fortune cookies invented ?

People in the United States of America seem to love fortune cookies. You've seen them eat it in many television shows and movies. It is basically a crispy dessert item that you break open to find a little piece of paper. The paper will have a sentence that tells you your "fortune" which is a prediction for the future.

The prediction has something like "You'll lose 20 dollars tomorrow", or, "You will find your love tomorrow". Fortune cookies are ordered in Chinese restaurants. But did you know that they were invented in the United States? People in California made it very popular in the 20th century.

you will be challenged

318 Are yes and no gestures the same everywhere ?

In the US, UK or India, when people shake their head left to right, they mean to say 'no'. When they nod their head up and down, they mean to say 'yes'. But in Albania and Bulgaria, the opposite is true. So, imagine if you visit Albania and shake your head left to right to a question, you're actually saying yes.

Such confusions in gestures confuse people when they travel or meet someone who has been using different gestures their whole lives. In the same way, the word 'no' or anything that sounds similar means 'no' in many languages except in the Greek language. In Greece, when you say 'ne' you mean 'yes'.

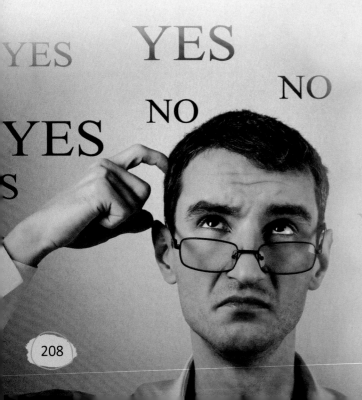

 **Do Americans eat a vegetarian diet?**

There were very few vegetarians in America. Just like most countries in Europe, most Americans loved to eat non-vegetarian food and had a diet filled with meat, dairy products and cheese. Then, fast food became more and more popular. Americans began to eat more fast food than regular food. The portions of fast food got bigger while the quality of fast food got worse.

Obesity and diabetes started affecting the population in much higher numbers. A food revolution was in order. That's when Americans began to adopt the vegetarian diet. About 4 per cent of the complete adult population now follows a fixed vegetarian diet which is about 7 million people.

That's a Stat!

0.5 per cent of the US population is vegan. Veganism is a diet that excludes meat and dairy products.

320 How do Americans like their coffee?

Another fun food fact about Americans is that they like their coffee with milk and sugar. That might not seem that great, but Americans are real coffee lovers. Several varieties of coffees are available here. Famous coffee franchises have been started in America and then have spread to different parts of the world. Also, USA imports coffee from many different places thus allowing there to be a wide range of coffee.

About 37 per cent of the total coffee drinking population take their coffee with milk and sugar. On the other hand, 21 per cent of the people prefer their coffee black, which means that it is served without cream, milk or sugar.

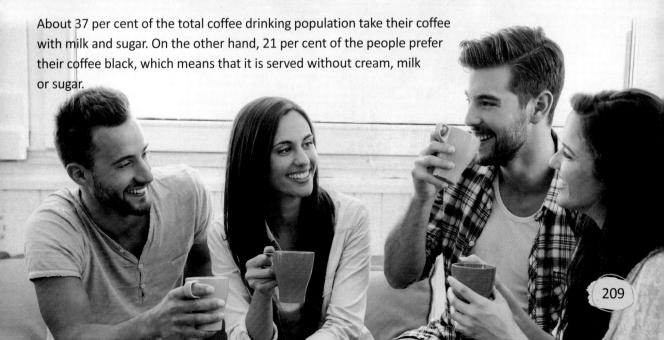

321 Do all gestures mean the same thing in different countries ?

The chin flick is a non-verbal gesture that you can see when you go to Europe. It is a gesture where a man or a woman brush the back of their hand underneath their chin. The motion ends with a flicking action.

In Belgium, Tunisia and Italy, this gesture is meant to cause offence. It is used to mean 'get lost' but implies an even ruder word of the language. It is also used to imply that the person doesn't care about who they are speaking to.

That is why, if you make this gesture in Belgium, you would probably cause offence. On the other hand, in France this gesture is a symbol of manhood and is performed by men with healthy beards. If you are ever confused, just avoid making the gesture to feel safe.

There are similar gestures like 'the fig' that mean something else in Turkey and something else in the US. In America, parents play a fun game with their children where they pretend to grab their nose and then make a fist with the thumb slightly out. They show it to a baby as proof. A similar game is played in the UK and Canada. But this game is never played in Turkey.

322 What does a tongue click mean in the Balkans ❓

In Bosnia and Croatia, tourists will witness people clicking their tongues often. It is also seen in places like Turkey and Greece. People click their tongues, make a small, sharp sound and indicate that they are saying no. Such non-verbal gestures are considered lazy or even rude in other countries, but they are casual and common in the Balkans.

Some even toss their head as they click their tongues. This added gesture is meant to indicate that they don't have something or to reinforce their earlier gesture to mean rejection. In the countries that use these gestures, there is no disrespect meant. People think that it's endearing, comforting and even friendly.

323 What is the moutza ❓

The moutza is a gesture which is used in Mexico, the Middle East, Africa and Greece. In this gesture, people raise their open palm out and spread their fingers out in front of someone. It is a way to indicate that they are unhappy. It is one of the oldest gestures used in the world and was used even in very old times like during the ancient Byzantium era.

During ancient times, soldiers would tie criminals to donkeys and drag them out in the public, so that the locals could surround them and shame them. They would even use the excrement from the donkeys and rub it on the criminals with an open palm.

324 What does it mean to cross your fingers in Vietnam?

If you cross your fingers in most places in the world, it would mean that you are asking for good luck. People cross their fingers and even their toes for luck. But that's not what it means in Vietnam, where crossing your fingers before a person means you are insulting them.

Crossing the fingers implies you are calling them a bad word and don't wish them luck at all. It is used by people who are arguing to communicate that they are fed up. Surprisingly, Vietnam is one of the few places in the world where crossing your fingers is a bad thing.

325 Are onomatopoeias common in all languages?

Onomatopoeias are words that indicate the sounds that are made by animals or moving objects. The train goes 'choo! choo!'. The crow goes 'caw! caw!' These sound words are called onomatopoeias. But there are different onomatopoeias used in different countries for the sounds made by different animals.

In the English language, bees go 'buzz! buzz!'. On the other hand, the bees in Afrikaans go 'zoem-zoem'. The cats say 'meow' in English, while they go 'meo' in Vietnam, 'nau' in Estonia and 'ngiau' in Malay. That is because our language influences how we hear and interpret sounds. So, onomatopoeias are different in all languages.

That's Just Weird

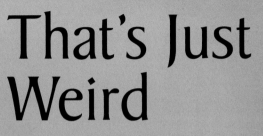

The answers to some questions in the world, give us a deeper understanding of history. Others explain science. But the world we live in can also be whacky and confusing. So, there are some questions that are just weird and their answers even more so. Let's read some weird facts!

326 How many ants are there on Earth?

The number of ants on Earth far exceeds the number of humans on the planet. For each person on the planet, there are 1.6 million ants. So, imagine, if one person decided to adopt ants proportionally, they would need 1.6 million of them!

This also indicates that the number of ants in this world is 1.6 million times the world population. The funny thing is that even then, their total weight is the same as the total weight of humans. That's because ants are tiny. Remember, there are different species of ants that vary in size and colour.

327 Can you burn calories by banging your head against a wall ?

At times when you just cannot find a solution to a problem, you feel like banging your head against the wall. Although, this action is never ever recommended as a solution, you will be surprised to learn that by banging your head, you are possibly burning 150 calories an hour.

There are several such bizarre actions that help you burn calories. Blinking is an exercise that can burn 2 calories per blink. Even laughing is a very healthy exercise, and it can help you burn up to 100 calories an hour. Especially if the joke is very funny. However, a bit of advice, don't give up exercising to try these.

328 What is the longest time between twins being born ?

When someone says twins, they mean to say two babies that were born on the same day to the same parents. However, did you know that there were miracle twins that were born 87 days apart from each other?

A woman named Maria Jones-Elliott gave birth to her twin girls Amy and Katie. Amy was born first, then Katie arrived three months after Amy. Their birth has been recorded in the Guinness Book of World Records. Amy was born earlier than the due date and had to be placed in an incubator, while her mother waited for her sister to be born. It was a stressful wait, but now both babies are happy.

329 Can you change your own lightbulb in Australia?

Not unless you are an electrician. It is an absurd law, but apparently, in Victoria, Australia, only qualified electricians can change light bulbs. It is just a simple action of switching off the power, turning the bulb out and twisting it in.

The second-most populated state in Australia, provides plenty of work for its electricians as the citizens are not allowed to change their own used light bulbs. So, what happens if you are in Victoria, sitting in the dark because a light bulb has gone out, and you need to change it? If it is known that you have broken the law, then you have to pay a fine of 10 Australian dollars.

330 Did a man fake his death to get out of a cell phone contract?

That is what happened in the United States of America when a man named Corey Taylor faked his own death to get out of a long-term contract with a mobile provider named 'Verizon Wireless'. He was very tired of receiving poor service and dropped calls. Besides, he would even had to pay 175 US dollars to cancel the contract.

So, to get out of the contract, he decided to act like he was dead. He prepared a fake death certificate and sent it to the company from a friend's fax machine. All of this because he wanted to avoid paying the compensation fees for ending the contract early.

I AM NOT ALIVE

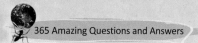

331 Do people have tongue prints ?

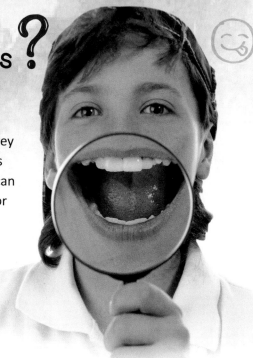

You can check out your own tongue print by sticking it out of your mouth and inspecting your tongue. All human beings have a thumb print. In the same way, they also have a tongue print. The tongue is an organ that is unique to each person. It is so unique that its texture can be looked at as unique information that can be used for identification verification.

Most ID verification is done using a biometric machine. A machine to identify the tongue is still under work, and those who believe in tongue ID verification think that there are many advantages to the machine being used.

332 Does light travel at the speed of light ?

No. Light can travel slower or faster than the standard time set for light to travel, which is 299 792 458 minutes per second. The slowest speed at which light has travelled according to scientific records is 38 mph. Light, is commonly believed to travel at a constant speed but it can change its speed.

No matter what the speed of light might be, at the constant speed, it is so fast, that were human beings capable of travelling at that speed, they would be able to circumnavigate the globe seven and a half times in one second. At a regular speed of 800 km per hour, a person would take 50 hours to circumnavigate Earth.

333 Can a whale be lonely?

There is a whale in the North Pacific Ocean that is called 'lonely' by scientists. It has attracted a lot of interest from scientists because they have been recording its song for two decades. They have never seen what the whale looks like. What is unique about the whale's song is that it is abnormally high-pitched.

A whale usually sings a song to get a response and to attract a mate. The reason scientists have called this whale 'lonely' is because it has an abnormal high-pitched voice which has failed to attract a response from other whales. So, it has been singing for the past 20 years without results.

Scientists think it is a fin whale. Fin whales are said to sing at 17 to 18 hertz. That is too deep for humans to hear without machines. But this whale's voice has been recorded at 52 hertz which is very unusual. The singing was picked up by the US Navy who began recording the song since the 1980s. The US Navy was attempting to pick up sounds from submarines in the North Pacific. The lonely whale's sound was heard by a Dr William Watkins in 1989.

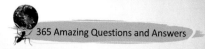

334 Who was the first man to urinate on the moon?

The first man on the moon was Neil Armstrong who travelled to the moon on Apollo 11. He set off to the moon on July 16, 1969 with Edwin 'Buzz' Aldrin and Michael Collins. They were the other two astronauts on the mission.

Neil Armstrong was the first man who stepped on the surface of the moon. It is said that nobody remembers the second man on the moon who was Buzz Aldrin. But he himself broke a record. It is said that he was the first man to urinate on the moon. He spoke about his achievement in a documentary called *In the Shadow of the Moon*, in 2007.

335 Who invented the smiley?

A man named Harvey Ross Ball is said to have invented the smiley face about 50 years ago. He was a man from Worcester in Massachusetts. They were classified as emoticons, in 1982, on a mail written by Scott Fahlman. But before him, a man named Vladimir Nabokov nearly invented the smiley.

He was giving an interview to a newspaper called The New York Times in April 1969. He made a comment when asked "How do you rank yourself among writers?". He replied saying that there should be a special typographical sign that authors use for a smile. It should be a concave mark with a 'supine round bracket'.

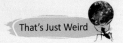

336 Can people have blue skin?

There once lived a man named Benjamin Stacy who frightened all the doctors when he was born. He had blue skin at birth. As soon as the doctors saw this, they rushed him to the University of Kentucky Medical Centre. During the treatment, the doctors found out that this blue skin colour went back generations.

Six generations before Benjamin, Martin Fugate settled in Eastern Kentucky near 'Troublesome Creek'. After him, many people from the family had skin that was tinged with blue colour. The Fugate family were suffering from a genetic condition called 'methemoglobinemia'. It is a rare condition that is passed on from generation to generation and can even survive marriage.

The condition is a blood disorder where the body produces more methemoglobin (a form of haemoglobin), than is necessary for the body.

This rare disorder could be acquired when a person is exposed to harmful drugs through their food or water.

That's a Stat!

A person has less than 1 per cent of methemoglobin. If they have 10 to 20 per cent, they are likely to have blue skin. At 20 per cent, they could suffer from heart abnormalities.

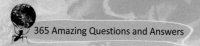

337 What is the oddest place for a post box ?

In every country, the postal system is very complicated. The big reason for its success (and failure) is that people live in the oddest places. Which is why, there are post offices in some strange places. One of the strangest places in the world is Susami Bay in Japan. This bay is 10 m under water.

That is right! It is an undersea post office. The population of this town has just about 500 people. But its post office has made it into the Guinness World Records. Every year there are about 1000 or 1500 pieces of mail dropped off in this post office.

338 Can a dead person win a race ?

Yes! Depends on the type of race, though. Back in 1923, a dead man named Frank Hayes won a horse race. He was a jockey. He had a horse named 'Sweet Kiss'. On June 4, they entered a race at Belmont Park in Long Island.

While the race was in progress, the jockey had an intense heart attack and died. But, his horse crossed the finish line with him still on his back and thus won the race. Hayes dropped out of the saddle and lay dead on the floor and could not collect his prize. It is probably the only time that a dead person won a race.

339 Is it expensive to keep minting pennies and nickels ?

Pennies and nickels are used in the US currency system. They are both expensive to mint. To mint a penny it takes 1.8 cents, which is a little more than twice its value. Nickels have a value that is half their minting price. A penny is made of zinc and a nickel is made of copper.

Strangely, even though they are such a loss, they continue to be minted. The people in the USA are against using pennies as they are petty change. In fact, it annoys them to be given pennies or nickels. So, even though minting pennies and nickels have been causing losses since 2006, they continue to be minted to this day.

340 Does cheese have maggots ?

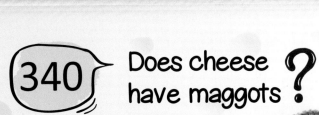

Have you heard of Casu Marzu? It is a cheese from Sardinia, a big island in Italy. Casu Marzu literally translates to 'rotten cheese'. It is also known as 'walking cheese'. The strange thing about this cheese is that it has live, moving maggots. How is this cheese made?

First, the cheese is soaked in brine. Then it is smoked and left out to ripen in 'Cheese cellars'. Most cheese makers leave it uncovered and out in the open. They allow flies to lay eggs on it. When the eggs hatch into white maggots, the tiny maggots feed on the cheese, and produce the enzymes that start the fermentation process and fatten up the cheese.

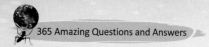

341 Did the HMS Trident have a pet reindeer?

World War II was a serious time. But there were some moments that were just weird. In 1941, the crew of the HMS Trident was gifted a reindeer by the USSR Navy. They named it Pollyanna and allowed it to stay on for six weeks with the crew.

The space that the crew had for themselves was already limited, but they adjusted to allow the reindeer enough space. The Russian crew had given them the gift, because the captain of the British HMS Trident, complained of his wife's problem pushing her pram in the snow. That is why the Russian admiral sent them a reindeer to make things easier.

Gifted by USSR Navy

342 Can a frog swallow its prey with its eyes?

A certain kind of frog, called the 'northern leopard frog' can swallow a prey with its eyes. This was proven after lots and lots of tests on the northern leopard frog! Apparently, the frog blinks many times to push its food back to the oesophagus. It mostly feeds on small creatures like the cricket which has an average size of 1.5 cm.

The frog can either blink, then swallow or even blink and swallow at the same time. When the frog finds its prey, it opens its eyes wide. Then it stares at the prey to confuse it. It flicks out its tongue and pulls the prey into its mouth.

343 — Can you trip over your own beard?

Yes! If it is long enough, you could trip over your own beard and even die! That is what happened to a man named Hans Steininger, who had a beard that was 1.4 m long, i.e., 4.5 feet. He died when he tripped over his own beard.

On regular days, Hans would roll up his beard into a pouch made of leather. For some reason, he did not do that, and that very day a fire broke out in his town. He was forced to evacuate and in his rush, he stepped on his own beard and broke his neck. The fire eventually got to him as well.

344 — Can a place have no roads?

There are no roads in a village named 'Giethoorn'. It is a Dutch village in the Netherlands where all the buildings are connected by footbridges and canals. The footbridges are made of wood. They add beauty to the canals that connect the local houses and shops. If you bring a car to this village, you will have to leave it outside.

Giethoorn is a very popular tourist spot. It reminds people of Venice which is another place that has canals connecting important places. People can tour the city on a canal tour and even take up cycling on the footbridges. Sailing is an important past time as well.

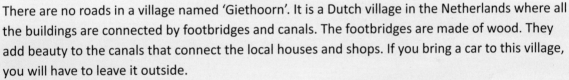

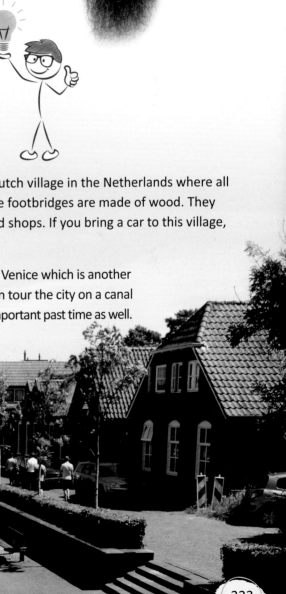

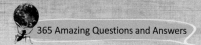

345 Can policemen use props?

Policemen have to behave themselves when they are on duty. But that doesn't mean that they cannot have fun. A man named Bob Geary requested permission to patrol and do his duty as a police officer while carrying a ventriloquist dummy. He named it 'Brendan O'Smarty'. He used the dummy to make children who were lost, smile, and make them feel comfortable.

Bob Geary would even pull out the dummy when he had to answer calls of domestic dispute. He apparently did so to lighten the serious mood. He was allowed to carry his dummy without a problem until his station received complaints.

That is when Officer Geary decided to act, and he spent nearly 10,000 dollars to get about 10,000 people sign a petition allowing him to carry his dummy. For this, he started an initiative on the ballot. He went around campaigning in the neighbourhood during the election season.

So, while regular politicians were promising to feed the poor and get more jobs, Officer Geary was promising to entertain everyone with his ventriloquism skills. His neighbours and friends were on his side when he went to campaign. Even people who were strangers used to flock to his side and support his initiative. Tourists would admire him as well.

That is probably why Officer Geary won his campaign so easily.

I will entertain everyone with my ventriloquism skills.

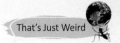

346 What is a chimera ?

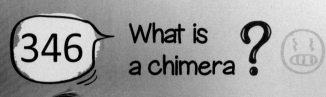

A chimera is a weird and rare genetic disorder where a person is declared as a 'mix' of two people. This means that if a mother is expected to have twins, there is a very small possibility that the material of the twins fused together in the womb to form one child. So, the child is a mix of the original and the twin.

What is strange is that people don't notice this at birth. Usually, people find out about such things when they take tests. A mother who had taken her daughters for treatment took genetic tests, and the results came back to say that she was not their real mother. But she had given birth to them. The doctors soon found out that she was a chimera.

347 How did Sigurd the Mighty die ?

In possibly the biggest example of 'karma' that the world has seen, a powerful man named Sigurd the Mighty was killed by the man he had murdered hours ago. Sigurd the Mighty lived during the 9th century when times were very different from today. He got his name from his powerful duels against his enemies.

Sigurd the Mighty was an earl from Orkney. He beheaded and killed a man. Then he carried the man on his horse's saddle. But something about that day was not right, because a tooth from the dead man's head grazed Sigurd the Mighty and took his life.

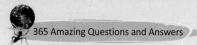

348 Can a glacier spill blood?

No. But there is a glacier in Antarctica called 'Blood Falls'. It is very strange because it occasionally releases a red liquid. If you view it first hand, you will think there is blood flowing down the glacier. In fact, it looks like the ice around the glacier is melting.

The water is very salty. The salt is trapped about 1300 feet beneath thick ice. That is where microbes have made a home for themselves. They feed on the sulphur and iron compounds that they find in abundance there. This entire reaction is what causes the red colour of the water. The red colour is simply oxidised salty water.

349 What is the sound that melting glaciers make?

Melting glaciers make a unique sound. It is like the sound that melting icebergs make. This sound is called 'bergy seltzer'. It is a unique fizzing noise that you would expect from a melting glacier. It sounds like a crackling, frying sound which you hear on a pan while making fries.

This sound was picked up by sailors on submarines when they were travelling near icebergs. This sound is also called the ice sizzle. The sound is said to be made by the air bubbles released from the melting ice. Peter Scholander was the first person to discover the sound. His discovery of how the sound was made helped put to rest several questions within the scientific community.

350 Does the Eiffel Tower move?

To understand the answer to this question, you must first know what the Eiffel Tower is made of. The man who designed it, Gustave Eiffel, chose to use iron to make the Eiffel Tower. He made this decision because iron has great resistance. He said that iron is 10 times more resistant than wood and 20 times more resistant than stone.

He knew that the Eiffel Tower would be a special structure that needs to last long, so despite the rust that iron goes through, he chose to use iron to make the Eiffel Tower. The Eiffel Tower now has much smaller supports and foundations than such a construction would have required had other materials been used. Gustave Eiffel also felt that the load on the foundation of the tower would not be great if he chose iron.

Here is something weird...the Eiffel Tower sways slightly in a storm. A storm hit the tower in 1999, and the Tower moved about 13 cm from its original position. Another reason the Eiffel Tower moves is because of heat. The Tower is constantly exposed to the heat of the Sun through the day and the afternoon. When the temperature is high, it affects the part of the Eiffel Tower exposed to the Sun. This part expands slightly. Even the portion in the shade might expand over time, but the one exposed to heat will expand faster and to a greater extent. The tower leans by 18 cm to get out of the Sun.

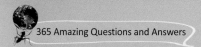

351 — How many times can a person be struck by lightning?

A man named Roy C Sullivan was struck by lightning seven times. He was a park ranger who worked for the maintenance of Shenandoah National Park. He had been working there for 43 years. When he was still new at the park, he was painting the wall of a bedroom when a storm began.

He was scared and hid between two beds to protect himself from the storm. That is when he was struck by lightning the first time. Then, after the seventh time, he made it to the Guinness Book of World Records as the person who has been struck by lightning the most times in the world.

352 — Do bacteria live in hairspray?

Yes, they do. Back in 2008, scientists found a new type of bacteria that live in hairspray. The bacteria were rod-shaped and seen as a contaminant in hairspray. It was a type of microbacterium that is quite unique. When they discovered the bacteria, the first aim of the scientists was to find out what the importance of such bacteria was.

In fact, it is weird and rare to find contaminants in hairspray, but some products do encourage the growth of bacteria. Similar bacteria were found in food items like cheese, milk, eggs and beef. They were even found in the blood of patients who had leukaemia.

353 Can you watch an opera from another country?

Yes, and you don't need the Internet to do it. There is a weird opera house called 'Haskell Free Library and Opera House'. It is very unique, because it is located on the border between USA and Canada. The stage is in one country, and half the audience sits in the US and the other half in Canada.

The opera house hosts both English and French entertainment for its audience, because a majority of the Canadian population speak French. It has been declared a Heritage Building, which means that special permissions need to be taken while making any changes to the building.

That's a Stat!

The Haskell library is open to the public of both countries and has more than 20,000 books in both French and English!

354 Did people use urine to whiten their teeth?

Over the course of history, researchers have found many strange uses for urine. Before the Industrial era, workers used to strongly believe in the 'cleaning powers' or urine. It was said to be corrosive. People have also linked it to generating electrical power.

Stem cells that were harvested from urine have been reprogrammed into neurons. They have been used to grow human teeth. In ancient Rome, people collected urine in vessels and used it to wash their dirty clothes to get rid of the stink. They even used it to whiten their teeth. Many people today believe that this worked. However, today we know that urine does not whiten the teeth.

355 What happened during the laughter epidemic?

Have you heard of the Tanganyika Laughter Epidemic of 1962? It was no laughing matter! Laughter is not just a sign of joy and happiness. After 1962, researchers realised that people could also laugh when they are distressed or angry about something. It is considered to be a sort of mania when they laugh.

The Tanganyika Laughter epidemic started in a girls' school. The girls began to laugh maniacally and couldn't stop themselves. Somehow, this epidemic spread to people outside the school so that 1000 people were affected during the epidemic. As a response, 14 schools were closed until the matter was resolved.

Doctors think this case is an example of psychological illnesses that are caused by chronic stress. It might have started with one girl in the first school who gave in to a fit of laughter. The laughter might have been a response to days of stress and anxiety without relief.

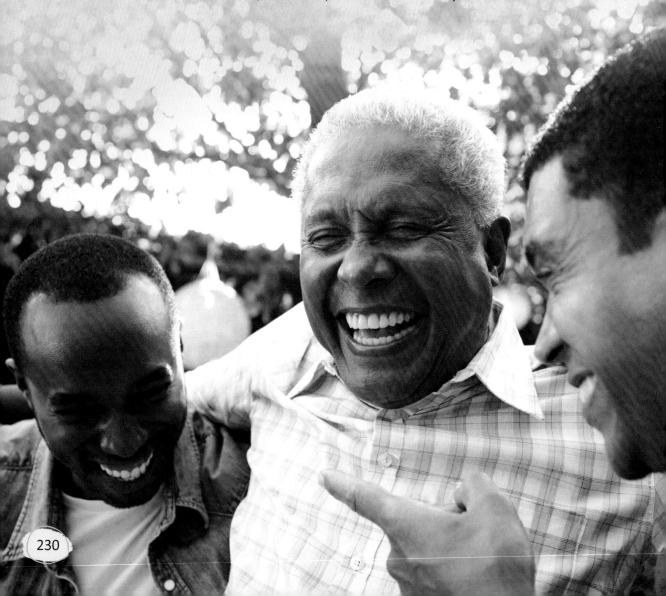

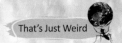

356 — How big is the largest snowflake?

The largest snowflake recorded is said to be 15 inches in diameter and 8 inches thick. This snowflake was recorded in the Guinness Book of World Records. But what is strange is that the size of the snowflake is just by word-of-mouth. A ranch owner named Matt Coleman of Fort Keogh claimed to have seen and measured this snowflake.

The snowflake fell in 1887, and he quickly pulled out his measuring tape to take a closer look. He said that the snowflake was larger than the milk pans he used in the 1800s. We cannot be sure if his snowflake was really that large, but we can be sure that snowflakes of that size existed.

357 — How big can an ant colony be?

An ant colony can be big enough to be called a mega-colony of ants. There is said to be a single mega-colony of ants that is slowly conquering the world. The colony is formed by Argentine ants which is a species of ants. They live across Europe, USA and Japan – that is three continents! They are a part of an inter-related colony.

Usually, ant colonies when they come in contact with each other could begin to fight. These Argentine ants do not fight each other. Argentine ants first came from South America and travelled the world because of human beings. One colony of Argentine ants now scales 6000 km.

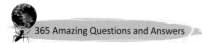
358 Was there a musical instrument made of cats ?

You might have seen Internet videos of cats playing musical instruments. Maybe such a musical cat was the inspiration for 'The Katzenklavier' which is an organ made of cats. It is also called the cat organ. In this instrument, eight cats were put into eight different cages. These cages were closely packed together. Then, a keyboard was attached to the back. Their tails were pinned to a key and pulled tightly.

When a person pushed on a key, it would slam a nail onto a cat's tail and the cat would meow in pain to make a sound. Obviously, this instrument existed way back in time in the 1600s. Today, this would be considered animal cruelty.

359 Can parasites help rats get over their fear of cats ?

There is a tiny, microscopic parasite called 'Toxoplasma gondii'. This parasite reproduces inside the stomach of a cat. But, it has unique ways of getting there. It might not naturally live in a cat's stomach. Instead, sometimes these parasites infect rats.

How do they get into the cat's stomach then? They work on the rat to make it less scared of cats. The rat becomes brash and bold, and the cat easily catches its prey and eats it up. The crafty parasites then make their happy way to the cats stomach where they reproduce in large numbers. Isn't that a unique way in which nature works?

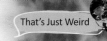

360 — Who was Colonel Mad Jack ?

'Mad Jack' Churchill was a colonel who fought in World War II. He was a British soldier. He was considered a great warrior by his mates. He had commanded his company. When he was wounded, he spotted a German soldier. Instead of being scared, he remembered his medieval bow and claymore sword that he had insisted upon taking with him to battle.

He killed the enemy soldier with his longbow. This was the only British soldier recorded to do so in World War II. What makes this story even more unique is that Mad Jack had been hit by a German machine gun. That is the kind of technology that was available for use during the war.

361 — Who was the first to film a toilet being flushed ?

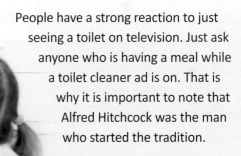

People have a strong reaction to just seeing a toilet on television. Just ask anyone who is having a meal while a toilet cleaner ad is on. That is why it is important to note that Alfred Hitchcock was the man who started the tradition.

He was the first man who showed a toilet being flushed in his film *Psycho*. The film was unique, and it is still remembered for many reasons. But, what is important to know is that it challenged the censor board of the movies at the time. They did not like to show things that were grotesque or...gross. And *Psycho*, showed both these in abundance.

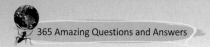

362 Can fruit flies become drunk ?

Some fruit flies are resistant to getting drunk. In fact, getting drunk is next to impossible for them because of their own genes. But this is only possible for them when they have an inactive 'happy hour gene'. This gene makes them sensitive to alcohol.

Scientists tested out this theory in labs where they exposed fruit flies to drugs that have an effect on their system. After getting drunk, the fruit flies would have periods of hyperactivity and experience a lack of coordination. Scientists think that if they are successful in reproducing this happy hour gene, then they might be able to find a way to cure alcoholics.

363 How old is the Oxford University ?

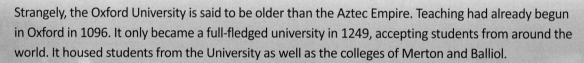

Strangely, the Oxford University is said to be older than the Aztec Empire. Teaching had already begun in Oxford in 1096. It only became a full-fledged university in 1249, accepting students from around the world. It housed students from the University as well as the colleges of Merton and Balliol.

It isn't, however, as old as the Nalanda University in India, which is said to be the oldest university in the world. But Oxford is one of the oldest universities that is still under operation. The Aztec civilisation only began 196 years after the Oxford University. The White House of USA is older than the ancient civilisation.

364 — Does it rain diamonds on Jupiter and Saturn?

Scientists think that it rains diamonds when rain gathers in the clouds upon Jupiter and Saturn. Diamonds are formed from highly compressed and heated carbon. Jupiter and Saturn have dense atmospheres that exert a lot of pressure and generate lots of gravity. This large amount of pressure and heat can squeeze carbon in mid-air creating diamond rain.

That is why scientists believe that both Jupiter and Saturn have lots of diamonds in their cores. There might be diamonds in the cores of Neptune and Uranus as well which are gas giants. Saturn experiences many storms, and it is possible that this is the time when it has the most diamond rain.

365 — Is Humpty Dumpty an egg?

If you read the nursery rhyme *Humpty Dumpty* you will notice a strange thing. No where in the rhyme has it ever been mentioned that Humpty Dumpty is an egg. But if you look at any illustration of Humpty Dumpty you will notice that the character is drawn as an egg. Why is that?

The first publication of Humpty Dumpty was included in *Juvenile Amusements* by Samuel Arnold. He published it in 1797. In the 17th century, the term Humpty Dumpty was first used and referred to ale and also to a short and clumsy person. But because it isn't right to show children, alcohol or injured people, illustrators began to draw eggs.

OTHER TITLES IN THIS SERIES

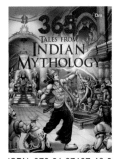
ISBN: 978-81-87107-46-0

ISBN: 978-93-52760-95-4

ISBN: 978-93-84225-31-5

ISBN: 978-93-80070-79-7

ISBN: 978-81-87107-53-8

ISBN: 978-93-83202-81-2

ISBN: 978-93-52764-06-8

ISBN: 978-93-80069-36-4

ISBN: 978-81-87107-52-1

ISBN: 978-81-87107-57-6

ISBN: 978-81-87107-58-3

ISBN: 978-93-80070-84-1

ISBN: 978-93-80070-83-4

ISBN: 978-93-84225-32-2

ISBN: 978-93-81607-49-7

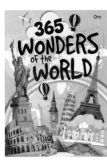
ISBN: 978-93-80069-35-7

ISBN: 978-81-87107-55-2

ISBN: 978-93-84625-92-4

ISBN: 978-93-85031-29-8

ISBN: 978-93-52760-96-1

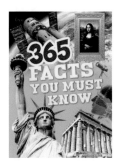
ISBN: 978-93-84225-33-9

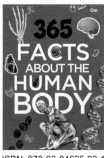
ISBN: 978-93-84625-93-1

ISBN: 978-93-84225-34-6

ISBN: 978-81-87107-56-9

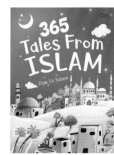
ISBN: 978-93-52764-05-1